TAB Property Guide

2005/06

Sandra Gannon, Jill Kerby

Eagle House, 14 Wentworth, Eblana Villas, Dublin 2.
Telephone: (01) 6768633 Fax: (01) 6768641

This book has been prepared as a general guide for use in the Republic of Ireland and is based on our understanding of present law and practice. While every effort has been made to ensure accuracy, neither the publisher nor editor are liable for any errors or omissions.

Published by

TAB TAXATION SERVICES LTD.

Eagle House, 14 Wentworth, Eblana Villas, Dublin 2.

Telephone: (01) 6768633

E-mail: tab@eircom.net

Web Site: www.tab.ie

ISSN No: 0790 9632

ISBN No: 0-9543730-3-0

Produced by Siobhain Usher & Catherine McGuirk

TAB Taxation Services Ltd.

Printed by Typeform Ltd., Dublin.

Sandra Gannon

Co Author TAB Property Guide / TAB Guide

Director of TAB Taxation Services

Jill Kerby

Co Author TAB Property Guide / TAB Guide

Personal Finance Columnist with the Sunday Times

Forward

Buying and investing in property has become such an important part of our lives that it is increasingly important that everyone from first time buyers to experienced investors have a good working knowledge of the subject.

For the past 20 years the TAB Guides on Money, Pensions and Tax have provided Irish consumers with a comprehensive account of every aspect of personal finance, from basic savings accounts and social welfare entitlements, to tax liabilities and retirement planning. A considerable amount of space has also been devoted over the years to mortgages and property investing and it has become a TAB topic that deserved its own Guide.

This book tries to answer as many of your property questions as possible and we hope it will be as useful for first time buyers, as it should be for people buying a second home, a buy-to-let or commercial property.

More importantly, we hope the information in this new Guide helps you to avoid making expensive mistakes and takes some of the stress and complexities out of the buying and selling process.

Sandra Gannon & Jill Kerby

Acknowledgments: We'd like thank permanent tsb, Gunne Residential, the Financial Regulator and the Revenue Commissioners for their help and co-operation in the preparation of this book.

Table of Contents

The 2005 TAB Guide to Property

Property ownership is an integral feature of the Irish psyche and explains not just why we have one of the highest home ownership ratios in the world at over 80%, but also our confidence in the investment property market for longer term personal wealth creation.

There are three reasons why most people think property is a good investment:

- Buying property has been, for most people, the only way to borrow large amounts of money cheaply.
- Rapid increases in property values over the years.
- Tax incentives relating to property investment.

If you buy a property for €300,000 cash and watch its price rise by 3% in real terms each year for the next 20 years you will discover that after 20 years the property will be worth €541,800 in real terms with a clear profit of €241,800 (after accounting for inflation).

If as many buyers are doing today, however, you decide to borrow €270,000 of the €300,000 purchase price instead and rent the property, and the rent covers the loan and expenses over the 20 years, your experience will be very different. The original €30,000 stake is now worth €541,800 and your new profit is not just €241,800, but €511,800. Because your original investment was low, your stake has increased by a factor of 18 in real terms (€541,200 ÷ €30,000). That's a good investment by any standards.

The ups and downs of property prices

Although property prices have steadily increased in this country over the past 30 years, the increase has not always been consistent as the following table illustrates. The example is an average, three bedroom semi-detached house in a typical Dublin suburban neighbourhood..

Average price of 3 bed semi, Dublin.

Year	€
1975	€10,500
1985	€55,000
1995	€120,000
2005	€360,000

Average price of 3 bed semi, outside Dublin.

Year	€
1975	€7,500
1985	€40,000
1995	€75,000
2005	€290,000

(Source: Insignia Richard Ellis Gunne Research)

Affordability the key

With interest rates still at historic low levels, the issue of long term affordability is crucial for first-time buyers and for buy-to-let domestic and commercial property investors who have access to cheap capital and long repayment periods.

Nearly 77,000 new homes were built in Ireland in 2004 and the serious supply crisis of recent years has receded. The Irish market is maturing, which is why the old adage about 'location, location, location' is still crucial when buying a property. This book provides simple guidelines and even some statistical data that will help you to make up your mind about the merits of the property you are considering well before you raise the mortgage and sign the deeds.

Residential and commercial property investors also need to keep the location of their property uppermost as it will impact on both the rental stream and capital appreciation. They need to ensure that they take extra care with overseas property purchases where the legal and tax regimes will differ from those at home. Meanwhile, older people who are considering buying a property for their retirement need to take into account issues like good access to public transport, and amenities like retail and health services in the new location.

Not everyone will own the bricks and mortar in their property outright: investment property funds, sold by life assurance companies and specialist fund managers are another property option. Substantial returns in recent years have rewarded investors, many of whom have used them to spread investment risk and to balance out pension fund and other savings portfolios.

The use of worked examples and case studies throughout this guide are also aimed to provide clear, easy to understand information that will give you the clearest picture possible of all the costs, and potential profits that you might accrue from your property investment.

1

Buying a home

For most people buying a home is their single, biggest investment and it can be an anxious time, especially if the property market is experiencing a boom, as it has in Ireland over the last decade, and you are afraid to miss the property boat if you delay your purchase.

Most people set off looking for a home based on how much they think they can afford, and this will often be determined by the size of the rent they are already paying, or their existing mortgage, as well as the location they favour. Taking a flexible approach to the latter however, may make it easier to stay within budget, but ultimately your lender will determine the size of your mortgage, based on the information you have provided about the property, your income and their assessment of your capacity to service the loan.

Everyone would like to own the house of their dreams, but this is not always practicable: a city property may cut down on commuting time, but it may not have a garden or garage and might be too small for a growing family. A suburban property might provide the space, but it might be too far from work and lack satisfactory amenities. Access to public transport, shops and schools are often cited as the three most important buying features after size. Each of them plays a part in establishing the market value of any property, something you need to consider even at the buying stage.

Raising finance

To buy a home, you need some capital, usually at least 10% of the purchase price. Banks and building societies are usually prepared to lend up to 90% mortgages, or 92% in certain cases, but better interest rates may be available to buyers who have more than 20% of the purchase price.

If an average new home costs €250,000, you will need €25,000 as starting capital, plus the cost of any searches, surveys, legal fees and mortgage indemnity bonds. These costs – see page 12 – should also be provided for by your savings, and not from borrowings. Stamp Duty because it can be such a substantial sum (see page 12) is usually incorporated as part of the mortgage loan.

Most savers of first homes usually choose a good, interest-yielding account in the post office, bank, building society or credit union to start the process, though you do not need to be saving with any particular institution in order to secure a mortgage with them at a later date.

Once you have the appropriate minimum capital you should shop around for the best mortgage. One way to start is to look at the updated and 'best buy' mortgage interest rate tables in the national newspapers. These include a column that shows the cost per thousand euro borrowed so that you can quickly calculate the monthly repayment of the mortgage size that you have in mind.

Using a broker

Another way is to use a mortgage broker or advisor who can match your circumstances with the right product and best interest rate on the market. They will help you fill out all the paperwork and explain all the costs and charges and explain the financial consequences, for example, of taking out a longer repayment term.

Many brokers also offer a low cost legal conveyancing service, which can substantially reduce the total purchase cost.

Brokers receive commissions from the lending institutions for sending your money their way. This usually amounts to 1% of the mortgage value (though the commission can be smaller for low volumes of referrals). In the case of a €250,000 loan, the commission can amount to €2,500. With such substantial commissions being earned, you should avoid dealing with mortgage brokers who ask for up-front arrangement fees, especially where they are not fully refundable.

Fee-based mortgage brokers and advisors usually refund all or part of the commission the lender offers them back to customer; this is because they are already receiving a fee for their work. This arrangement can provide good value indeed where the legal conveyance cost is also included.

Your credit rating

When you apply for a loan, the bank or building society require information about your income, employment, living costs and existing loan repayments to help them decide whether you can afford to repay a loan.

The lender will also look at your credit rating. If you have a good history of repayment on previous loans you will have a positive credit rating. Your credit rating may be poor and considered "impaired" if you missed repayments on a regular basis or failed to pay off a previous loan.

If your have an impaired credit rating, it may be difficult for you to get a loan, though special impaired credit mortgages are available at premium interest rates which can go as high as 7% per annum.

When you apply for a mortgage most lenders in Ireland will do what's known as a "credit check" on you. This credit check is done through the Irish Credit Bureau (ICB), who hold information about borrowers and their loans for 5 years after the loan is closed.

The information held by the ICB about each borrower includes .

- Your name, date of birth and address.
- The names of lenders and account numbers of loans you currently hold, or
- that were active within the last five years.

- Repayments made or missed for each month on each loan.
- The failure to clear off any loan.
- Loans that were settled for less than you owed and
- Legal actions your lender took against you.

This information is sent to the ICB from the lenders when you take out a loan.

If you want to see the information that's held about you can apply to

The Irish Credit Bureau
ICB House
Newstead
Clonskeagh
Dublin 14
Tel No 01 2600388.

The cost of obtaining this information is €6.

How much can I borrow?

All lenders require certain income conditions before they will extend finance and a rule of thumb is that the loan must not exceed up to four and a half times your income. If you are joint applicants, the limit might be up to three and three quarter times the combined income, depending again on your income level. A self-employed person will usually need to provide proof of average taxable earnings over the past three years. A couple earning €40,000 and €30,000 respectively can expect to borrow up to €262,500 in total.

Lenders are expected to 'stress test' a mortgage before it is approved and this involves either reducing your income levels – say, cutting in half the second salary to simulate the loss of income that might happen if you started a family and one partner only worked part-time. The lender should also calculate the cost of the loan if interest rates were to rise by at least two percent.

For example, a more typical €250,000 mortgage loan at 3.25% interest would cost €1,212 per month stretched out over a 25 year term. If interest rates were to rise to 5.25%, the repayments would rise to €1,480 per month or an additional €3,216 per annum. Over a 25 year period, instead of the entire mortgage costing €363,600 it would cost €444,000 at the higher interest rate.

Adequate stress-testing is also important if you are considering raising a second mortgage on your property;

- in order to buy a holiday home or second property; or
- if, as a retired person, you are considering a home equity release loan (see page 32) , which does not have to be repaid during the owner's lifetime, or
- the outright sale of a part of the value of your home to a residential reversion company.

Joint ownership

Not everyone can afford to buy a property on their own, or may have a partner or spouse with which to share the cost. Instead, they may have a like-minded sibling(s) or friend(s) who are also keen to exchange their rent book for an affordable home of their own. The cost of a €1,212 monthly mortgage repayment (i.e. a €250,000 loan) split four ways is eminently more 'do-able' than one person having to make that payment, and lenders are perfectly happy to extend homeloans to joint buyers.

However, the key to a successful joint loan application is a clear exit strategy if one of the buyers decides, or is forced (through illness or redundancy) to liquidate their share. A good solicitor can draw up a contract that will be acceptable to lenders and buyers and satisfy everyone's need for total transparency. It is also very important that the joint owners draw up a Will, naming whoever it is that inherits their share of the property. Death-in-situ will need to be addressed, just as redundancy, illness, emigration, marriage has been.

Joint Ownership Case Study

Morgan, Louise and Jack are a brother, sister and best friend who are all in their late 20s and have been sharing an apartment successfully for the past three years. Their rent is now €1,400 a month plus contents insurance of €60 per month which they split three ways. The three each have €10,000 in savings/inheritance and the €30,000 is more than sufficient for a down-payment on a €275,000 apartment plus the cost of legal and other fees and some furniture. As first time buyers there is no Stamp Duty on the property as it does not exceed 125 square metres. Their new €250,000 mortgage costs €1,082 per month over 30 years or €361 each; the annual management fee of €500 a year costs them €14 each a month; mortgage protection and contents insurance now costs each of them a total monthly outlay of €40.

Morgan, Louise and Jack agreed that if any of the partners become redundant or ill, with no reasonable chance of re-employment within six months or if anyone marries, or emigrates, the other two will be obliged to buy out their share at market value. If that cannot be agreed, the property will be put up for sale. They have each written wills with Morgan and Louise leaving their shares to each other. Jack wants to leave his share to his parents, but with the proviso that it is then offered for sale at market value to the other two. Their solicitor must now examine this agreement and if it is in order, submit it to the lender.

No one expects the siblings and their friend to live together forever, but if they keep the apartment for the required five years to qualify for the Stamp Duty exemption (see page 12), and the property grows in value by 6% per annum to €334,500, they could expect to walk away with about €20,000 profit each, doubling their original investment of €10,000.

Interest Rates

Choosing a lender that offers the best, long-term interest rates, is very important. By carefully shopping around, you may be able to save yourself a considerable sum of money over the term of your loan. No lender will guarantee that their rate will always be the most competitive, but certain lenders have better track records than others for offering consistently lower rates and charges. Check them out.

Below we illustrate the typical monthly repayments on a €250,000 loan, assuming annual interest rates of 3.25%, 4,25%, 5.25%, and 6.25% p.a. over four lending periods:

Monthly repayments - €250,000 loan				
Rate	**20 yrs**	**25 yrs**	**30 yrs**	**35 yrs**
3.25%	**€1,412**	**€1,212**	**€1,082**	**€ 991**
4.25%	**€1,537**	**€1,343**	**€1,218**	**€1,133**
5.25%	**€1,668**	**€1,480**	**€1,362**	**€1,282**
6.25%	**€1,802**	**€1,623**	**€1,511**	**€1,439**

The longer your mortgage term, the cheaper the monthly repayment will be. But when the total cost of interest and capital repayments are added up, an extra five or ten years will cost you thousands of extra euro over the entire term. As the table on the next page shows, the total cost of the €250,000 loan can range hugely depending on both the interest rate and term of the loan.

Total cost of €250,000 loan				
Rate	**20 yrs**	**25 yrs**	**30 yrs**	**35 yrs**
3.25%	**€338,880**	**€363,600**	**€389,520**	**€416,220**
4.25%	**€368,880**	**€402,900**	**€438,480**	**€475,860**
5.25%	**€400,320**	**€444,000**	**€490,320**	**€538,440**
6.25%	**€432,480**	**€486,900**	**€543,960**	**€604,380**

As the above table illustrates, anyone who arranges a 30 or 35 year mortgage would be advised to accelerate their payments after a few years, when their income has increased and the high early costs associated with home ownership have diminished. By reducing a mortgage from 35 years to 30 years, you will pay an extra €91 per month, but you'll end up paying €26,700 less in interest assuming a rate of 3.25%.

House purchase related costs

There are other costs besides the interest rate connected with home purchase and these include application or arrangement fees, legal and valuation fees, administration fees, indemnity bonds and Stamp Duty as well as the ongoing cost of insuring your home, furnishing it, and paying on-going utility and maintenance costs.

Stamp Duty

One of the most significant costs for buyers is Stamp Duty. Only first-time buyers buying new and second hand properties worth up to €190,500 are exempt from Stamp Duty.

Rates of Stamp Duty for second hand residential property

Value	First Time Buyers		Owner Occupiers
	Up to 1st Dec. 2004	**On/After 2nd Dec. 2004**	**(Not first time buyers)**
Up to €127,000	**Nil**	**Nil**	Nil
€127,001 - €190,500	**Nil**	**Nil**	**3.00%**
€190,501 - €254,000	**3.00%**	**Nil**	**4.00%**
€254,001 - €317,500	**3.75%**	**Nil**	**5.00%**
€317,501 - €381,000	**4.50%**	**3.00%**	**6.00%**
€381,001 - €635,000	**7.50%**	**6.00%**	**7.50%**
Over €635,000	**9.00%**	**9.00%**	**9.00%**

New houses or apartments not exceeding 125sq. metres in floor size are exempt from Stamp Duty provided the purchase is made by or on behalf of a person who will occupy the property as their Principal Private Residence for a five year period and no rent (other than rent under the Rent-a-Room Scheme) is derived from the property during this period.

If the property ceases to be your Principal Private Residence within these five years e.g. if you move and rent the existing property then a clawback of the full amount of the Stamp Duty will arise.

If you purchase a property in excess of 125 sq. metres and the property is occupied by or on behalf of a person as their Principal Private Residence for five years and no rent (other than rent under the Rent-a-Room Scheme) is derived from the property during this period, Stamp Duty will be payable on the higher of:

- The site cost

  or

- 25% of the total cost

Where a new house or apartment is purchased by an investor, Stamp Duty is payable on the entire amount paid for the property.

A first time buyer (FTB) is a person, (or where there is more than one buyer, each person)

- who has not on any previous occasion, either individually or jointly, purchased or built on their own behalf a house or apartment, in Ireland or abroad.

- Where the property purchased is occupied by the purchase or a a person on his behalf as their principal place of residence

- Where no rent other than rent under a Rent a Room scheme (see page 83), is derived from the property for five years after the current purchase. If rent is received with this five year period (other than under the Rent a Room scheme), then a clawback will arise. The amount of the clawback will be the difference between the Stamp Duty rates for new first time buyers and the amount of Stamp Duty paid as a first time buyer. This additional Stamp Duty will become payable when rental income is received for the first time.

Stamp Duty is also payable where the property purchased is occupied by the purchaser, or a person on their behalf as their only principal place of residence and where no rent (other than rent under the Rent-a-Room Scheme) is derived from the property for five years after completion of the current purchase.

There is no Stamp Duty on the mortgage document on properties valued up to €254,000. All mortgages worth more than €254,000 are subject to Stamp Duty of 0.1% to a maximum of €630.

A site transferred from a parent to a child, for the purpose of the construction of the child's principal private residence, is exempt from Stamp Duty (limited to one site with a value of €254,000 per child).

Legal fees

Home buyers can typically expect to pay between 0.75% and 1.5% of the purchase price of the property plus VAT in legal fees. The rule here however is to "shop around".

Competitive rates can be found from many solicitors who will charge a flat fee based on time and expertise rather than as a percentage. Others now work as part of a 'panel' of solicitors engaged by mortgage brokers and charge a flat fee. The legal conveyancing is part of the overall fee charged by the advisor. Because such advisors refund mortgage commissions which are typically 1%-1.25% of the mortgage value, the overall cost or arranging the loan and the conveyancing is much less than paying separately for such services.

> Conor and Sinead have bought a 10 year old house for €275,000. They have been quoted conveyancing fees of 1.5% of the value of the property plus €100 plus 21% VAT, the total charge will amount to just over €5,100. If however, the fee-based advisor charges, say €3,000 to arrange the loan of €247,500 (i.e., €275,000 minus the 10% downpayment) and then refunds a 1% commission (i.e. €2,475) received from the lender, the borrower could end up only paying in the region of €500 to arrange the mortgage and conveyancing, a huge savings on the conventional cost of this service that they were quoted earlier.

Mortgage indemnity bond

If you borrow more than 70% - 75% of the value of your home, you may also have to pay a Mortgage Indemnity Bond from the bank or building society. These bonds guarantee the total repayment of your loan in the event of your home being sold for less than the outstanding loan amount. Indemnity bonds usually cost 3.5% of your borrowings above the specified limit and, while the cost can be absorbed into your mortgage term, it is more cost efficient over the longer term to pay it at the outset.

The following is a typical list of charges you could pay when buying a €250,000 home with a mortgage of €225,000. (Assuming you are a first time buyer).

	€
Application Fee (Where applicable)	**€60**
Search Fees	**€150**
Survey Fees	**€375***
Legal Fees (€3,750 plus 21% VAT)	**€4,537.50 ****
Mortgage Indemnity Bond	**€1,313**
Mortgage Registry Fee	**€131**
Land Registry Fee	**€375**
Total Charge	**€6,941.50**

* Survey fees are often charged as a €1.50 rate per €1,000 value, but can also be a flat fee.

**Assuming a 1.5% fee plus VAT of 21%

Land Registry / Registry of Deeds

It will cost you €131 to register your mortgage in the land registry. The cost of registering your ownership of the new property is based on its value.

Value of Property	Fee
Up to €13,000	€125
€13,000 - €26,000	€190
€26,001 - €51,000	€250
€51,000 - €255,000	€375
€255,001 - €385,000	€500
Over €385,00	€625

Insurance

The monthly mortgage repayment is not the only one you will have to make. Mortgage protection and buildings insurance are compulsory in most cases and can cost up to 10% of your gross monthly mortgage repayments.

Mortgage protection

Mortgage protection insurance is a life assurance policy that covers the value of the mortgage and ensures that your debt to the bank or building society is repaid in the event of your death or that of your spouse. Rates are based on age and sex and the premiums can be paid monthly or annually. You are not obliged to purchase the policy from the lender and you should shop around for the best market rate, especially if you are a smoker.

The cheapest form of this insurance is term cover, which can be arranged on a level or decreasing premium basis that reduces in tandem with the outstanding capital debt. Arranging the insurance on a decreasing basis is slightly cheaper, but the drawback is that although your benefits will clear your outstanding mortgage, there will be no extra cash available to ease any other financial burdens your dependents may face. By arranging your cover on a term basis, you will be guaranteed a lump sum (the size of the original mortgage) throughout the entire duration of your loan.

An increasing number of new home owners are arranging serious illness cover as part of their mortgage protection policy in order that the loan can be paid off not only if they die but also in the event of a life-threatening illness. The cost is higher, but can be mitigated by arranging the policy on a decreasing term basis.

Such a policy is recommended if one of the joint mortgage holders is not employed outside the home, and would not have access to an occupational Permanent Health Insurance (PHI) benefit also known as Income Protection Insurance.

Payment Protection Insurance is available to mortgage holders and, in the event of loss of income as a result of redundancy or illness will pay your mortgage premiums for a specific period. However, if you have adequate PHI cover, you may feel that it is unnecessary for you to take out Payment Protection Insurance as well. After all, the whole purpose of PHI is to provide you with a replacement income so that you can meet your regular outgoings and other financial commitments. Keep in mind, however, that most PHI policies only pay benefits after an average of 26 weeks have elapsed, while many Payment Protection plans pay out benefits after just one month of redundancy, illness or disability.

Mortgage Protection Case Study

Conor and Sinead have a mortgage of €250,000 over 30 years. They are both age 29 and non-smokers. The monthly cost of a Conventional Mortgage Protection Plan and a Mortgage Protection Plan, which included Serious Illness Cover for you, will work out approximately as follows:

Plan type	Monthly cost €
Conventional Mortgage Protection Plan	€21
Mortgage Protection Plan plus Serious Illness cover	€166

**Available from all the major lenders, this insurance costs about €4.50 for every €100 cover required per month and pays out benefits if you become ill or disabled and are unable to work, or have been made redundant. You need to have been out of work for about 30 days before your first claim can be made and there is generally a 12 month payment limit per claim. Payment protection insurance is not cheap, and if you already have Permanent Health Insurance or serious illness cover, it may be unnecessary.*

Insuring your home and contents

Your home and its contents are among your most valuable possessions. Insuring them against fire, theft and other damage should be an important priority. If you have a mortgage you will be required to take out compulsory buildings insurance, which varies in price depending on the size, location and rebuilding cost of your property. Your lender requires this insurance, not for your benefit, but for theirs as their priority is to protect their financial interest in the property.

The minimum insurance you require is the cost of rebuilding your home in the event of its destruction. Your rebuilding costs are not the same as your mortgage amount, or the market value of your property. If you have any doubt about the rebuilding cost of your property you should arrange for an independent valuation or survey. Take care not to underinsure your home or contents because most home insurance policies include what is known as an "averaging" clause which determines that if you underinsure your property, for example, by 50%, the insurer is only obliged to pay you 50% of your claim.

Most general insurance companies offer combined buildings and contents policies. Some automatically provide contents cover worth up to half the value of the building cover. Engage an independent financial advisor to help you find the right policy for you and to help you make sure you have put a correct value on your fittings and personal belongings. Premium discounts may be available, which will depend on your age, whether the house is occupied during the daytime and if it is fitted with approved locks, fire and burglar alarms etc.

You are not legally obliged to buy buildings and contents insurance from your lender though they will be happy to offer you a policy. If you use a mortgage broker who offers to arrange the policy, make sure to ask to see a price comparison table. You should also ensure, once your mortgage is paid off, that your building and contents are properly valued and insured.

The Financial Regulator publishes a bi-annual home insurance survey (see www.itsyourmoney.ie) which shows the considerable difference in charges between home insurers for typical properties around the country. The following case studies of a five bedroom detached house in company Offaly and a one bedroom apartment in Dublin shows just how competitive insurance rates can be:

Insurance Case Study

"My home is a 5 bedroom detached bungalow in County Offaly. The rebuilding cost is €240,000 and the contents are worth €40,000."

Is the area liable to flooding?	No
Is the area prone to subsidence?	No
Age of property:	35 years
Age of applicant:	40 years+
Claims experience:	No
IS199 Burglar alarm fitted:	No
Neighbourhood watch scheme:	Yes
Security locks fitted on doors and windows:	Yes
All risks (unspecified items):	€1,000

Quotation	Broker / Direct	Quotation
Allianz	Direct	€386* (contents cover €48,000)
AXA	Direct	€637
Eagle Star *Note 1&3*	Both	€612
Ecclesiastical	Both	€749
FBD *Note 2*	Both	€390 (contents cover €48,000)
Hibernian	Direct	€564 *
Quinn Direct	Direct	€463
Royal & Sun Alliance *Note 3*	Broker	€692
Simply Mortgages *Note 3*	Direct	€442 (contents cover €65,000)

* premiums include all risk cover of €2,000 for Allianz and €3,900 for Hibernian

Source: IFSRA Home Insurance cost survey March 2005

Note 1 Premiums automatically include all risk cover of €1,275 when contents cover is selected.

Note 2 Premiums include accidental damage on buildings cover only

Note 3 Premiums include accidental damage cover

Insurance Case Study

"My home is a 1 bedroom apartment (rented accommodation) in Dublin 11. The contents are worth €40,000.

Is the area liable to flooding?	No
Is the area prone to subsidence?	No
Age of property:	7 years
Age of applicant:	28 years*
Claims experience:	No
IS199 Burglar alarm fitted:	No
Neighbourhood watch scheme:	No
Security locks fitted on doors and windows:	Yes
All risks (unspecified items):	None

Quotation	Broker / Direct	Quotation
Allianz	Direct	€175
AXA	Direct	€236
Eagle Star (note 1, 2)	Both	€153
Ecclesiastical	Both	€333
FBD	Both	€140
Hibernian	Direct	No Quote
Quinn Direct	Direct	€183
Royal & Sun Alliance (note 2)	Broker	€178
Simply Mortgages	Direct	€117 (contents cover €44,500)

* Male and female renting the accommodation for the last 2 years. No previous contents insurance held.

Source: IFSRA Home Insurance cost survey March 2005

Note 1 Premiums automatically include all risk cover of €1,275 when contents cover is selected.

Note 2 Premiums include accidental damage on buildings cover only

Note 3 premiums include accidental damage cover

Title insurance

Under our current legal system, all property transactions, whether for the purchase of a new house, or the simple remortgaging of your existing home, is treated as a full conveyancing transaction. Unfortunately for someone who wants to remortgage, this means unnecessary cost and delay as their solicitor goes through the same lengthy process of seeking title deeds, examining the title, contacting the new lender to tell them that the title deeds are acceptable and then waiting for their reply before seeking the mortgage cheque. Inevitably you will wait four to six weeks and pay the same conveyance fee – between 0.75% and 1.5% plus VAT – unless you can negotiate a flat fee.

Fortunately, Title Insurance, which was first launched here in 1998 cuts through much of the red tape of remortgaging as the insurance company takes the risk, and not the lender, if any difficulty arises with the title.

With title insurance the deeds do not have to be checked and the lender does not have to confirm that the title deeds are acceptable, allowing the mortgage cheque to be available in as little as five working days from when the lender issues its mortgage offer.

Title insurance is available from at least six major mortgage lenders and costs up to €999 regardless of the value of the property.

Choosing a mortgage

Once you have found the property you want to buy, have established with your lender or broker how much you can afford to borrow, and have worked out all the additional purchase costs – like the Stamp Duty, search, survey and legal fees and the compulsory insurance – you now need to decide what type of mortgage to buy. The type of mortgage can impact on the amount you pay both in both the short and longer lending term.

Annuity mortgage

The annuity method, also known as a repayment mortgage, is the most common way to pay off a mortgage. Annuity mortgages involve the payment each month of interest and some of the principal of the loan. In the early years, the bulk of the payment is interest, which will be the subject of mortgage interest tax relief at source.

As the years progress, you will pay less interest and more capital until eventually your entire loan will be cleared. A typical repayment mortgage will be repaid as illustrated on page 11 over a 20 year term.

In the tax year 2005 a first-time buyer will benefit from tax relief at source to the tune of €1,477 in the first year on a typical €250,000 mortgage (€7,388 @ 20%), while other mortgage holders will benefit by €1,016 (€5,080 @ 20%). This tax benefit will decrease each subsequent year as the amount of mortgage interest payable decreases.

Endowment mortgage

After revelations about high costs and charges back in the early 1990s, the sale of endowment mortgages, which combines a home loan with a life assurance policy, collapsed in Ireland. Theoretically, the monthly contributions into the endowment investment (ideally a with-profits policy that locks in annual growth) would grow sufficiently over the course of the loan to repay the original mortgage amount.

The lack of transparency in the sale of these products, high charges, reduced tax relief and market volatility showed just how poor value these products were and only a tiny proportion of mortgages are now arranged in this way. Most existing endowment mortgage holders have discovered that in order for their loan to be repaid at maturity, they must either increase their contributions or hope for a surge in stock market performance.

Now referred to as 'investment' mortgages, only investors with considerable confidence in the stock market and who arrange these loans on a nil-commission, low cost basis should consider buying one.

Pension mortgage

Pension mortgages are an attractive and tax efficient method of purchasing property. In addition, as a result of the Finance Act 2004 and changes in the Revenue Commissioners' practice pension arrangements, you can now borrow to acquire assets for investment purposes, giving rise to what is termed Geared Property Pensions.

Both pension mortgages and geared property pensions are particularly attractive where an individual may wish to use their pension to purchase a commercial property or 'buy to let' residential property. See Chapter 4 for an example of how a pension mortgage works.

Interest only mortgage

Interest only mortgages are usually only available to property investors, such as buy-to-let purchasers who intend to sell the property within 10 or 15 years, using the capital appreciation to pay off the original borrowings. The attraction of such a loan is that large amounts of capital is not tied up, but depending on the borrower's financial position, the lender may require a lower loan to value borrowing ratio and may also require other loan security. (see Chapter 4)

Current account mortgage

Available from only a few lenders, this mortgage combines your variable rate repayment and your current account balance in a way that automatically reduces the outstanding capital of your mortgage. The money that is normally left in your current account for day to day expenditure, plus any additional savings you may wish to add to the account (all account balances 'earn' the equivalent of your mortgage interest rate) are used against the daily outstanding mortgage value. This day to day adjustment results in tiny slivers of capital being repaid sooner, and future interest payments on those slivers being avoided. Over the course of the loan, there is substantial interest savings. Meanwhile your account continues to act as a normal current account.

Cheque book mortgage

This mortgage provides the borrower with a book of cheques, which can be used to make purchases (minimum amounts apply) borrowed against the built up equity in your house. The amount you can borrow depends on the size of your equity. This is a very convenient facility, as the amount borrowed via the cheque book is repaid at the low mortgage rate, rather than a higher personal loan rate. But it also requires some discipline since the temptation is to use this cheap finance for less than necessary purchases.

Variable or fixed rate?

Should you arrange your mortgage on a variable interest rate basis or fix the interest for a period of years? Nearly all new borrowers are offered a discounted fixed rate for the first year of their loan, which usually amounts to a saving of a couple of hundred euro. In year two, you immediately revert to the variable rate of interest, which can go up and down over the term of the mortgage.

A fixed interest rate can provide considerable peace of mind and protect the borrower from the volatility of world money markets, but you can also suffer financially - if rates fall and your rate is fixed at a higher level for a few more years. The cost of breaking a fixed rate mortgage can be very high. Some banks charge nearly the entire interest balance that they could have expected to earn if you had seen out the contract.

Repaying a €250,000 annuity mortgage

End of year	Annual repayments	Capital repaid	Loan outstanding at end of year	Interest paid	Mortgage interest relief (granted at source)	
					First time home buyers	Other home buyers
	€	€	€	€	€	€
1	14,383	6,727	243,273	7,656	1,531	1,016
2	14,383	6,938	236,335	7,444	1,489	1,016
3	14,383	7,157	229,178	7,226	1,445	1,016
4	14,383	7,382	221,796	7,001	1,400	1,016
5	14,383	7,614	214,182	6,769	1,354	1,016
6	14,383	7,853	206,329	6,530	1,306	1,016
7	14,383	8,100	198,229	6,283	1,257	1,016
8	14,383	8,355	189,874	6,028	1,206	1,016
9	14,383	8,617	181,257	5,765	1,153	1,016
10	14,383	8,888	172,369	5,494	1,099	1,016
11	14,383	9,168	163,201	5,215	1,043	1,016
12	14,383	9,456	153,745	4,927	985	985
13	14,383	9,754	143,991	4,629	926	926
14	14,383	10,060	133,931	4,323	865	865
15	14,383	10,377	123,554	4,006	801	801
16	14,383	10,703	112,851	3,680	736	736
17	14,383	11,039	101,812	3,343	669	669
18	14,383	11,387	90,425	2,996	599	599
19	14,383	11,745	78,680	2,638	527	527
20	14,383	12,114	66,566	2,269	454	454
21	14,383	12,495	54,071	1,888	377	377
22	14,383	12,888	41,183	1,495	299	299
23	14,383	13,293	27,890	1,090	218	218
24	14,383	13,710	14,180	672	134	134
25	14,417	14,180	0	241	48	48
Total	359,609	250,000		109,608	21,921	18,814

Assumptions:

Interest Rate 3.1% *(typical first time buyer rate)*

Gross Repayments €1,198 p.m. or €14,383 p.a.

Mortgage Interest relief is for a married couple in 2005.

Refinancing debt with a mortgage

One of the by-products of the property boom has been the high amount of equity that has been built up in Irish homes, equity that some owners use to finance other investments, or that can be called upon to help reduce other debt, such personal loans, credit card balances, hire purchase contracts.

By refinancing expensive, double digit debit like personal loans, hire purchase contracts or credit cards, onto an existing mortgage of 3.25%, the borrower can drastically improve their monthly cashflow.

The danger with refinancing other debt this way is that short-term borrowings become long term borrowings. The interest rate at which the non-mortgage debt is now being paid may have dropped, but instead of being paid off over the usual personal loan or hire purchase period, say, three to five years, it is being stretched out over the remaining years of the mortgage.

In too many cases, the borrower may also opt to lower their total repayments even further by reverting back to the original mortgage term of 20 or 25 years (see page 12). This has the effect of further lowering total monthly mortgage and loan payments, but at a considerable price. As the following example shows, the cost impact of this strategy can be quite high as the total interest payment over the extended mortgage period soars. This cost will go even higher if interest rates go up at any point in the term of the new mortgage.

Original mortgage and personal loan plans					
Loan	**Amount owing**	**Term remaining**	**APR**	**Monthly payment**	**Cost of Credit**
Existing mortgage	€50,000	20 years	3.25%	€282.40	€17,775
Home improvement loan	€18,000	4 years	8.45%	€440.61	€3,149
Hire purchase loan	€10,000	3 years	10.75%	€323.87	€1,659
Total loans (A)	€78,000			€1,046.88	€22,583

New 'refinance' loan plan					
Loan	**Amount owing**	**Term remaining**	**APR**	**Monthly payment**	**Cost of Credit**
Existing mortgage				€282.40	€17,775
Home improvement loan				€115.15	€8,676
Hire purchase loan				€61.75	€4,823
New refinance plan (B)	€78,000	20 years	3.25%	€459.30	€30,603
Additional cost of refinance plan: (cost of credit (B) minus (A))					€8,020

Local authority loans

Record numbers of houses have been built in recent years, but many people have been priced out of the house market, especially in Dublin.

Shared ownership loans are available from Dublin City Council and other Dublin area county councils to those on a single income who earned no more than €36,800 in the previous tax year (subject to applicants eligibility for inclusion in the scheme). In the case of a two-income household, two and a half times the principal income and once the second income must be less than €92,000. The maximum borrowing limit is €230,000 and the variable interest rate charged is currently 3.55% which includes mortgage protection cover of 0.598% The maximum price you can pay for a home under the shared ownership scheme is €250,000.

Shared Ownership Schemes are also operated by local authorities and for many they offer the first step in purchasing a home of their choice. In effect the local authority buys the home for the applicant. The applicant then acquires or takes out a mortgage from the local authority - minimum 40% / maximum 75% - of the property and pays rent to the local authority in respect of the remainder. For loans of €140,000 and over the share is on a 50/50 basis. The local authority's share or the rental element must be bought out within 25 years and can be bought out after a minimum of three years.

Home Equity Release Loans and Annuities

Equity release loans have grown in popularity in recent years, especially amongst older, retired homeowners whose properties may be worth a great deal, but whose pensions are not.

Three branded products now exist on the Irish market, a non-repayable fixed rate mortgage which is only repaid after the death of the borrower or if the house is sold or is left uninhabited by its owner for six months or more, and two annuity based products from SHIP and RRL Ltd., which purchase a portion of the house in exchange for a cash payment or regular, guaranteed income.

The fixed rate home equity bank loan product, is only available to people who are aged 65 and over and who own their own home. The 15 year fixed interest rate of 6.4% APR currently carries a hefty premium over and above the variable interest rate, although this gap could narrow if mortgage interest rates were to increase. You must borrow a minimum of €20,000 and no more than €250,000.

The amount that can be borrowed depends on the borrowers age and the value of the property:

Aged	%
65 - 69	Up to 20%
70 - 74	Up to 25%
75 - 79	Up to 27.5%
Over 80	Up to 30%

The annuity-based products are not loans, but involve the outright sale of a portion of the person's home in exchange for a payment that is based, not on the market value of the property, but on an actuarial formula which takes into account the borrower's age, sex and longevity risk.

The older you are – and sellers must be at least 70 and own the property outright – the higher the exchange price. There is no repayment involved in this product, but the seller must agree to exchange at least 50% ownership of the property to the buyer, remaining the legal owner of the balance of the property.

Borrowing against the equity value of your home can be a suitable way to enhance your income, but the compounding effect of the deferred interest on the outstanding capital – both of which must be paid eventually – means that your home will be worth less should you need to sell it, say, to pay for long term care.

The exchange of half the equity value of your home in the form of an annuity or cash, for less than market value, also results in you having a much diminished asset, unless there is considerable capital growth in the property to make good your loss.

How an equity release loan works

Seamus and Susan are age 75 and 73. They have modest pensions but are in good health. They own their home, which is worth €250,000 and they would like to draw down some cash to make some repairs, redo the garden and to enhance their own lifestyle. Under a bank equity release scheme they can 'borrow' €62,500 at a fixed rate of 6.4% APR over a 15 year period. In the course of the 15 years Seamus has pre-deceased Susan, but now, at age 88, she requires residential nursing care. The house must be sold. By the end of the 15 year period, the total repayment of both the original loan of €62,500 and the interest is €158,447. Without any capital appreciation, there would only be a balance of €91,553 from the proceeds of the sale. But assuming that inflation remains low, at say, a steady 3% per annum, and that Irish property prices match inflation, Seamus and Susan's property will be worth nearly €389,500. Once the original loan has been deducted, it is hoped that the new balance of slightly over €231,000 will be sufficient to meet Susan's financial needs.

Mortgage Interest Relief

Mortgage interest relief is available at source at the standard rate of tax only (20%). This means that your mortgage provider will reduce your monthly mortgage repayments by the amount of tax relief you are entitled to.

From 1st January 2004 first time mortgage holders, for the first seven years (five years prior to 1st January 2003) can claim 100% tax relief on the interest paid within the following limits:

- €8,000 for a married couple, who are jointly assessed for tax
- €8,000 for a widow(er)
- €4,000 for a single person

Non first time buyers can receive 100% tax relief on interest paid within the following limits;

- €5,080 for a married couple who are jointly assessed or a widowed person.
- €2,540 for a single person.

Bridging loan interest

Additional tax relief is allowed for interest on bridging loans obtained to finance the disposal of your main residence and the acquisition of another residence. This relief is confined to a period of 12 months from the date the loan is obtained. It is subject to the same restrictions as mortgage interest. However, both reliefs may be claimed at the same time.

Capital Gains Tax and Principal Private Residence (PPR)

No Capital Gains Tax arises on the disposal of your main residence and grounds of up to one acre, provided it has been occupied by you throughout the entire period of ownership. You are still deemed to occupy the residence where you are absent for any period of employment abroad or during absence imposed by conditions of your employment, provided you live in the house before and after the period(s) spent abroad. (See case study)

If your house was not your principal private residence for the entire period of ownership e.g. if you rented the house for a period, any gain arising on the sale of the house will be apportioned between the period when it was your principal private residence (PPR) and the period when it was not. The gain when it was your PPR is exempt and the balance of the gain is liable to CGT @ 20%.

For CGT purposes, certain periods of absence are regarded as periods of occupation such as the last 12 months of ownership and any period of absence throughout which you worked in a foreign employment or any period of absence not exceeding four years during which you were prevented from occupying the residence because of employment, provided you occupy the residence before and after the period of absence.

Brian and Eilis have decided to rent their home while they worked abroad. They have a mortgage of €85,000, mortgage interest of €4,800 p.a. and outgoings (agency fees, insurance, repairs etc.) of €1,600. They rent the house for €1,000 a month.

		€
	Gross Rental Income	€12,000
Less:	Mortgage Interest	(€4,800)
	Outgoings	(€1,600)
	Taxable income	€5,600

Tenants tax obligations

If you work abroad and rent your home, your tenant is obliged to deduct tax at the standard rate from the rental income and pay this tax over to the Revenue Commissioners. When you complete your Irish tax return, you will get credit for this tax.

This obligation on your tenant to deduct tax from your rental income is removed if you appoint an agent to look after your tax affairs here in Ireland while working abroad.

Comment: *If you work abroad, TAB can provide a comprehensive tax and financial advice service to minimise your tax obligations here while you work abroad.*

Case Study of CGT liability on Private Residence

Brian and Eilis bought their home in January 1992 for €50,000. They rented it out for four years from 1st January 2000 to 31st December 2003, while they worked abroad. The house was considered their principal private residence for eight years, from January 1992 to end December 1999. They sold it in December 2004 for €200,000. The house was considered their principal private residence again in 2004, and their total period of ownership was thirteen years with four years as non principal private residence. Their CGT liability is calculated as follows:

Brian & Eilis' position

		€
	Sale Price	€200,000
Less:	Selling Costs	(€2,000)
	Purchase Price	€50,000
	Indexation @ 1.406	€20,300
	Indexed Purchase Price	€70,300
	Capital Gain	€127,700
Less:	Capital Gains Exemption	(€1,270)
	Taxable Gain	**€126,430**
	Tax @ 20%	**€25,286**

Brian and Eilis may claim CGT exemption for the eight years while the property was their main private residence, together with the last 12 months of ownership which is deemed to be their Principal Private Residence. The CGT liability will be €7,780 (4/13 x €25,286). They could also claim total exemption from total CGT, provided they returned and lived in their former home for a period before selling it

Capital gains tax indexation factors

Year of purchase	Year of Disposal							
	97/98	98/99	99/00	00/01	2001	2002	2003	2004
1974/75	6.112	6.215	6.313	6.582	6.930	7.180	7.528	7.528
1975/76	4.936	5.020	5.099	5.316	5.597	5.799	6.080	6.080
1976/77	4.253	4.325	4.393	4.580	4.822	4.996	5.238	5.238
1977/78	3.646	3.707	3.766	3.926	4.133	4.283	4.490	4.490
1978/79	3.368	3.425	3.479	3.627	3.819	3.956	4.148	4.148
1979/80	3.039	3.090	3.139	3.272	3.445	3.570	3.742	3.742
1980/81	2.631	2.675	2.718	2.833	2.983	3.091	3.240	3.240
1981/82	2.174	2.211	2.246	2.342	2.465	2.554	2.678	2.678
1982/83	1.829	1.860	1.890	1.970	2.074	2.149	2.253	2.253
1983/84	1.627	1.654	1.680	1.752	1.844	1.911	2.003	2.003
1984/85	1.477	1.502	1.525	1.590	1.674	1.735	1.819	1.819
1985/86	1.390	1.414	1.436	1.497	1.577	1.633	1.713	1.713
1986/87	1.330	1.352	1.373	1.432	1.507	1.562	1.637	1.637
1987/88	1.285	1.307	1.328	1.384	1.457	1.510	1.583	1.583
1988/89	1.261	1.282	1.303	1.358	1.430	1.481	1.553	1.553
1989/90	1.221	1.241	1.261	1.314	1.384	1.434	1.503	1.503
1990/91	1.171	1.191	1.210	1.261	1.328	1.376	1.442	1.442
1991/92	1.142	1.161	1.179	1.229	1.294	1.341	1.406	1.406
1992/93	1.101	1.120	1.138	1.186	1.249	1.294	1.356	1.356
1993/94	1.081	1.099	1.117	1.164	1.226	1.270	1.331	1.331
1994/95	1.063	1.081	1.098	1.144	1.205	1.248	1.309	1.309
1995/96	1.037	1.054	1.071	1.116	1.175	1.218	1.277	1.277
1996/97	1.016	1.033	1.050	1.094	1.152	1.194	1.251	1.251
1997/98	-	1.017	1.033	1.077	1.134	1.175	1.232	1.232
1998/99	-	-	1.016	1.059	1.115	1.156	1.212	1.212
1999/00	-	-	-	1.043	1.098	1.138	1.193	1.193
2000/01	-	-	-	-	1.053	1.091	1.144	1.144
2001	-	-	-	-	-	1.037	1.087	1.087
2002	-	-	-	-	-	-	1.049	1.049
2003	-	-	-	-	-	-	-	1.000
2004	-	-	-	-	-	-	-	1.000

Owner Occupier in a Designated Area

In 1986, areas were designated in each of the five cities - Cork, Dublin, Galway, Limerick and Waterford. Areas are designated by order of the Minister for the Environment and Local Government, with the consent of the Minister for Finance under the Urban Renewal Act, 1986. These Urban Renewal Schemes were subsequently extended to include areas in many of Ireland's major towns.

1994 Urban Renewal Scheme

The 1994 scheme was more focused than its predecessor, concentrating on those areas where dereliction was most severe and providing for greater remedial works and measures to conserve existing urban infrastructure. More emphasis was placed on residential development in inner urban areas to provide a better mix of social and private housing and a greater use of vacant upper floors.

1999 Urban Renewal Scheme

Following an in-depth consultancy study on the operation of urban renewal schemes, the Government introduced a major new urban renewal scheme in 1999. The scheme, which benefited five cities and thirty-eight towns represented a more targeted approach to urban renewal incentives, concentrating not just on areas of physical development but also on issues of local socio-economic benefits.

The termination date was extended to 31st July 2006 in respect of the 1999 Urban Renewal Scheme, provided 15% of the total project cost had been incurred by 30th June 2003. Application for certification must have been submitted to the local authority by 31st July 2003 and certification must have been issued by 30th September 2003.

Town Renewal Scheme

Town Renewal Schemes are based on a similar approach to that which applies in relation to the 1999 Urban Renewal Scheme. Designations are based on Town Renewal Plans (TRPs) which in turn were based on the principles of promoting the physical renewal and revitalisation of towns, enhancing their amenities and promoting sustainable development patterns. The termination date for Town Renewal Scheme has been extended to

31st July 2006 provided full planning application has been received by the relevant planning authority by 31st December 2004.

Rural Renewal Relief

This relief was introduced in the 1998 Finance Act. It designated parts of Cavan, Roscommon and Sligo and the administrative county of Leitrim and Longford.

The deadline for the Rural and Urban Renewal Schemes for tax relief for expenditure on commercial, industrial and residential projected has been extended to 31st December 2004. The termination date for rural renewal relief was extended to 31st July 2006 provided full planning application has been received by the relevant planning authority by 31st December 2004.

Designated Area Tax Relief

If you buy, build or restore a dwelling in a designated area, you are entitled to offset part of the development cost against your income for tax purposes. An annual deduction of 5% in the case of construction expenditure and 10% in the case of refurbishment expenditure may be claimed each year for 10 years. To claim this relief, you must be the first owner-occupier of the dwelling after its construction or refurbishment. You will not be entitled to this relief for any year in which the dwelling is not your sole or main residence.

The following are examples of the tax relief you may be entitled to if you buy and/or build or refurbish property in tax-designated areas. If you build in a designated area you will be entitled to a 5% deduction against total income for 10 years and if you refurbish a property, you will be entitled to a 10% deduction against total income for 10 years.

Building a new home

Michael built a new home for €300,000 in a designated area. The site cost was €40,000, his mortgage was €225,000, his income was €75,000 p.a.

	€
Purchase price	€300,000
Less: site cost	(€40,000)
Qualifying expenditure	€260,000
Annual Relief (5% of €260,000 over 10 years)	€13,000
Tax Relief @ 42%	€5,460

Buying a new home

Maire bought a new home for €275,000 in a designated area. The site cost was €35,000.

	€
Purchase price	€275,000
Less: site cost	(€35,000)
Qualifying expenditure	€240,000
Annual Relief (5% of €240,000 over 10 years)	€12,000
Tax Relief @ 42%	€5,404

This annual allowance will be granted at Maire's marginal rate of tax of 42%.

Inheriting/Bequeathing property

The family home is often the biggest single asset a person has to pass on when they die. If you have a holiday home or investment property, these valuable assets will also become part of your estate, to be divided up between your heirs.

In Ireland, Capital Acquisition Tax or CAT, is payable by the individual who inherits the asset. In some other jurisdictions, like the United States, estate tax is payable, after which the beneficiary inherits their share of the assets, tax-paid.

No CAT is payable on any assets in Ireland between legal spouses. However, CAT must be paid when an asset is received by other categories of beneficiaries, such as children, grandchildren, siblings, cousins and by people who are not related to each other, such as friends or unmarried partners.

The exception to this tax liability is a shared family home where the parties have lived continuously together for at least three years and where the person who is inheriting the property (who can be a child, relative or 'stranger') does not own outright or a share of another property and does not dispose of the property for at least six years.

How C.A.T. exemption works

Paul and Anna have been living together for five years in a house they bought together which is now worth €450,000. Paul dies suddenly, but because he named Anna as the beneficiary of his half share of the property, and they had been living together continuously for at least three years, she will not have to pay any CAT on the €225,000 worth of the property that she has inherited from him. Had this CAT exemption not existed, Anna would have been obliged to pay €40,333 in tax on her share of their house. If Paul had not written a will, because he and Anna were unmarried, his next of kin, his parents, would have inherited the property, tax free. Anna will have to keep living in the property for at least six years to retain her tax exemption.

SUCCESSION ACT 1965	
Relatives surviving	**Distribution of estate where the deceased dies intestate**
Spouse and Issue	**2/3rds to spouse, 1/3rd to issue in equal shares.** **Children of a deceased son or daughter take their parent's share.**
Spouse and no Issue	**Whole estate to spouse.**
Issue and no Spouse	**Whole estate to Issue in equal shares.** **Children of a deceased son or daughter take their parent's share.**
Father, mother, brothers and sisters	**1/2 to each parent.**
Parent, brothers and sisters	**Whole estate to parent.**
Brothers and sisters	**All take equal shares.** **Children of a deceased brother or sister take their parent's share.**
Nephews and nieces	**All take equal shares.**
Remoter next-of-kin	**All take equal shares.**

Early inheritance

If you want to leave a property to someone after you die it is important that you write a will, clearly setting out your intentions. If you die without a will, or intestate, your property will become part of your estate's assets and will be divided up between your heirs under the terms of the Succession Act 1965, which is set out on the previous page.

The high cost of property, especially for first time buyers, has resulted in the phenomena of early inheritance. Some estate agents now say that perhaps as many as one in five of new home purchases are being made with some kind of parental financial assistance, often in the form of an early inheritance funded by an equity release from the parents' own home.

The following is the current tax-free threshold for CAT under the three categories of relationships. Inheritances and/or gifts received over and above these amounts are subject to 20% inheritance tax.

Group 1:	**€466,725 where the recipient is a child, or minor grandchild of the benefactor, if the parent is dead. In some cases this threshold can also apply to a parent, niece or nephew who has worked in a family business for a period of time.**
Group 2:	**€46,673 where the recipient is a brother, sister, niece or nephew or linear ancestor/descendent of the benefactor or where the gift is made by the child to the parent.**
Group 3:	**€23,336 in all other cases.**

High capital appreciation on family homes that may have been purchased 20 or 30 years earlier means that many parents are raising new or additional mortgages which they are then passing onto their children who then use this money as a down-payment on their first home. Parents who consider this kind of early asset transfer should keep in mind the following:

- Your present age and ability to repay the loan will determine how much you can borrow against the current value of your house and the length of the repayment term. If you are in your mid-50s for example, the lender may only allow you to borrow for a 10 year term, until age 65.
- What impact will this new loan have on your current lifestyle or, if you have been able to extend the loan past age 65 on pension income?
- Instead of making an outright gift of this money, consider asking your adult child to repay all or a part of the loan, factoring the repayments into their own monthly budget.
- If you 'gift" one child the price of a downpayment, can you afford to do this again with other children? Is favouring one child over another going to cause grief in the family?
- If you are already retired and you want to gift your adult child by way of an equity release loan that does not require repayment during your lifetime, (see page 32) keep in mind that if you live to an advanced old age, you may need to sell the property to pay for long term care. The capital debt will have to be paid off at that point, plus the interest that has been accruing for many years. You – and your children - could face a cash shortfall, especially if property values do not keep apace with the interest repayment.

Gifting second property

Parents who own a second property may opt to transfer ownership to the adult child(ren). However, not only will any value in excess of the CAT threshold be liable to 20% tax, but because the second property is not their principal private residence, the parent will also be liable for a Capital Gains Tax (CGT) bill of 20% of the value of the property over and above its original purchase price. Only the primary residence is free from CGT if it is sold or transferred to a new owner.

CGT Liability on Second Property Transfer

Donal and Nora are in their late 50s. They own a holiday home in Lahinch worth €300,000 which they decide to transfer to their two children who are keen to get on the property ladder. They bought the cottage in 1995 for a market value of €75,000. Gifting the value of the cottage equally to their children does not trigger a CAT bill because the value of the property is well below the €466,725 tax free threshold between a parent and child. But the sale of the property means that Donal and Nora are liable for capital gain tax because the cottage is not their private principal residence. The liability is €38,057, calculated as follows and takes into account capital gains tax indexation relief.

Donal and Nora's capital gain computation 2005

		€
	Sales Price	€300,000
Less:	Selling Costs	€9,000
		€291,000
Deduct:	Value on 6th April 1974 adjusted for inflation: i.e. €75,000 x 1.309	€98,175
	Capital Gain	€192,825
Less:	**CGT** Exemption x 2 as cottage is in both names	€2,540
	Taxable @ 20%	**€190,285**
	Tax Payable	**€38,057**

2

Buying a holiday home

The pleasure of finding yourself in your own holiday home on a beach, woodland or mountainside in just a few hours is, for many of us, well worth the additional expense and work. Keeping two houses is twice the trouble of just owning one, but in recent years, generous tax relief and capital appreciation has convinced thousands that a holiday home is also a very good investment.

When buying a holiday home you need to keep your guard up, however, and not allow your emotions to outweigh your good sense. You need to ask yourself exactly why you want a second home, and not confuse the pleasure you had staying in a rented property for a couple of weeks with year-round ownership. A second home, like a first one, has to be paid for, insured and maintained. It will suffer from wear and tear, utilities will add to the annual cost, the garden will need to be tended regularly and you will be liable for local service charges. The Revenue Commissioners will require you to file an annual tax return if you earn rental income when you and your family are not in residence.

If your holiday home is strictly for your personal use, then its location can be determined strictly by your personal tastes rather than the preferences of the wider holiday rental market. An isolated cottage high up in the Kerry mountains may not appeal to holiday visitors as much as a beachfront property, so keep this in mind if you hope to earn regular income from your holiday home.

The resale price of your property may be irrelevant if you intend for this house or apartment to remain in the extended family for generations. But even then you might want to consider that as your children grow older, they may not want to spend their holidays and weekends exclusively at the family cottage; selling it after a decade may be the more practical option. If that is a realistic supposition then you may want to consider the property's resale potential…before you sign the contract.

Raising the Finance

There are two principal ways to raise finance for a holiday home – by taking out a separate mortgage or by refinancing your existing property, if you have one, with what is known as an equity release loan.

Most lenders today will allow you to borrow up to 90% of the total amount of equity you own in your existing property to fund a holiday home, presuming, of course that they are satisfied you have the capacity, with or without rental income, to comfortably meet the repayments.

Refinancing the principal residence has become the most popular way to raise finance for those owners with sufficient equity, and it is usually cheaper than raising a separate mortgage. This is because the new property is being secured against the existing one. Others prefer not to risk their family home should they be unable to meet their repayments on the holiday home and opt for a completely separate mortgage, but they need to be prepared to pay an interest 'premium', usually in the region of 0.5%.

Equity release mortgages are also available if you buy your holiday home abroad, and many buyers find it easier and more convenient to deal with an Irish lender than a foreign one, where you may need professional assistance if you don't speak the language and are unfamiliar with their buying procedure.

Irish banks will not lend separate mortgages for overseas property because of the legal difficulties in collecting their debt – also known as foreclosing - if the owner falls hopelessly into arrears. However, one major bank, AIB, has a relationship with a Spanish bank to facilitate Irish loans.

How much can I borrow?

Sean and his wife Maura, who are both 50, own a house with a market value of €500,000. Their outstanding mortgage is €75,000 and their equity is worth €425,000. They want to borrow €275,000 to buy a cottage in the west. They earn a combined income of €80,000 a year, which is sufficient to repay the new remortgage of €275,000. In fact, the lender was willing to let them borrow up to 90% of the value of their home, or €450,000 at just 2.9%, their popular tracker rate. Had Sean opted for a separate loan, he would have been offered a 3.4% interest rate. At 2.9% the new €275,000 mortgage will cost €1,506 per month for 20 years, the maximum term the lender will consider. At 3.4% the loan would have cost €1,574 per month. By refinancing, using their existing home equity, Sean and Maura will save €16,320 interest over the course of the 20 year loan.

The same variety of mortgages are available to holiday home buyers as to first home buyers, and you will have to decide whether to opt for a variable, fixed or tracker rate and whether it is feasible to opt for an interest-only loan, or even a pension mortgage.

Your choice of lender might effect the kind of mortgage you take, since not every lender, for example, offers the popular new 'current account' mortgage, which speeds up the reduction of the loan by offsetting, on a daily basis, the sum in credit in your current account against the capital outstanding in the mortgage.

An interest-only loan is a lower monthly repayment option, since no capital is being repaid. For example, if a traditional capital and interest loan of €200,000 over 20 years costs a holiday home buyer €1,144 per month at a 3.4% interest rate, the monthly repayments for an interest-only loan of that size will cost €566 per month, presuming that the lender is willing to maintain the term for 20 years and accepts another asset as security (such as another property, shares or life assurance investment policy.)

If the term was reduced to 10 years, the conventional interest and capital repayment would be €1,964 per month, but as an interest only loan, would remain at €566 per month, you will still have the €200,000 capital to be repaid at the end of the 10 years.

Interest-only loans are usually aimed at investors who expect not just to rent their property, but who factor in sufficient capital appreciation in order to clear the loan and make a profit after a specific time period. An interest-only loan is therefore less suitable for a holiday home, especially one that is being bought using a family home as equity or security. Most lenders want to be satisfied that you have sufficient other assets (which might include a portfolio of stocks and shares, an investment policy, even a large pension fund) before they will lend an interest-only mortgage for non-investment purposes.

By using a broker with a wide range of agencies you should get a good selection of mortgage products from which to choose. A fee-based broker will usually refund any commission received from the lender that should mitigate costs like surveys, legal fees and even stamp duty.

If you have a mortgage, both the loan and your holiday home will need to be insured. The cost of the mortgage protection insurance will depend on the term of the loan, your age and state of health. (See Chapter 1 page 18) The cost of the buildings insurance will depend on your property's location, size, value and security.

If a new, single mortgage is taken out to finance the holiday home and your existing one, your insurer may allow you to top up your existing mortgage protection policy or will require that a new policy be taken out. This is where a good broker comes in handy as they can negotiate the best price for this cover.

Home and Contents

If you have a mortgage you are obliged to have building insurance. Your holiday home will need to be insured for buildings and contents separate to your existing property.

Most home insurance policies automatically include contents cover which is the equivalent of half the buildings value, but if your holiday home is only modestly furnished, you may not need the same proportion of insurance as your principal residence. Do a proper audit of the furnishings and contents to establish exactly how much it will cost to replace these goods in the event of damage or theft and then adjust your cover.

A homeowner with a high value existing property – i.e.. c.€750,000 and over – who then buys a holiday property might want to consider an inclusive insurance policy that also insures holiday homes, boats or mobile homes. These policies are usually better value than insuring the holiday home separately and in the case of at least one insurer, a survey is done for you of the buildings and contents thus ensuring an easy and accurate claims process.

Insure both houses separately or together?

Martin and Karen own their family home in Dublin worth in the region of €700,000. They also own a holiday home in Co. Galway that is worth €250,000. Both houses need to be insured. The contents insurance for the Dublin home is €150,000, but just €20,000 for the cottage.

The couple were quoted a range of prices for the insurance, on a separate and joint policy basis and even though the quotations for separate insurance was €110 cheaper for the holiday home, they opted instead to accept a joint quotation of €890 for the main house and €780 (instead of €670) from a well-known insurer.

"Our broker advised in the end that using a single company, which was prepared to assist in the quotation survey would save us time and stress in the event of a claim." Martin and Karen were surprised at how expensive it was to insure the cottage, but were told the premium price is due to the long periods in which it would be vacant and its remote location vis a vis the emergency services. Shopping around every year for a quotation should save them money, however.

Stamp Duty

One of the most significant costs for buyers of second homes is stamp duty. Only first-time buyers buying new and second hand properties worth up to €190,500, are exempt from Stamp Duty. If you buy a holiday home you will pay full rate Stamp Duty.

Rates of Stamp Duty for Residential Property

Value	First Time Buyers		Owner Occupiers	Investors
	Up to 1st Dec. 2004	**On/After 2nd Dec. 2004**		
Up to €127,000	**Nil**	**Nil**	Nil	Nil
€127,001 - €190,500	**Nil**	**Nil**	**3.00%**	**3.00%**
€190,501 - €254,000	**3.00%**	**Nil**	**4.00%**	**4.00%**
€254,001 - €317,500	**3.75%**	**Nil**	**5.00%**	**5.00%**
€317,501 - €381,000	**4.50%**	**3.00%**	**6.00%**	**6.00%**
€381,001 - €635,000	**7.50%**	**6.00%**	**7.50%**	**7.50%**
Over €635,000	**9.00%**	**9.00%**	**9.00%**	**9.00%**

Legal fees

The purchase of a second home requires legal conveyancing that must be done by a qualified solicitor. Conventional fees amount to 1% of the property value plus VAT at 21% but you should shop around for a better fee or consider arranging the purchase through a mortgage broker or advisor who includes conveyancing as part of their service package.

Buying costs add up

Sean and Maura's €200,000 holiday home, in which a 10% downpayment has been paid, will attract the following duties and fees. They may be able to reduce the legal and survey fees by shopping around.

- 4% stamp duty of €8,000.
- €2,420 in legal fees based on a rate of 1.5% of the property value plus 21% VAT.
- c.€60 application fee (this varies according to lender).
- €300 survey fee, based on a valuation of €1.50 per €1,000 purchase price.
- c.€150 search fee, usually charged as a flat fee.
- €375 land registry fee.
- €131 mortgage registration fee.

Total buying costs: c.€11,436.

Building your holiday home

Owning a site of land and then building a holiday home is another popular option for second home owners in Ireland, with many people returning to their native county. Seaside destinations are by far the most popular, but this is prime land and has become very expensive. While it is nearly always cheaper to build than to buy, labour costs are high and will also have to be factored into your budget.

Rigorous planning rules also mean that you must check with your local planning authority and its county development plan before you spend a penny building or even renovating your holiday home, especially if it is a listed building.

You will either need 'full planning permission' or 'outline permission' from your local authority. Full planning permission will require detailed plans for your proposed holiday home and you must not divert from this plan (or an existing plan if you have bought a site that already has planning permission) without making a new application. Outline planning permission, which usually lasts up to three years, means that the local authority has agreed 'in principle' to your project based on where it is based and the layout of the building work. To get full permission you will still need to present detailed plans.

The application process, which begins with you advertising your planned development and erecting a site notice, can easily take two months, and longer if someone submits an objection to the planning authority from where your application will go to An Bord Pleanala (www.pleanala.ie) for final consideration. You in turn can appeal to An Bord Pleanala if your application is refused by the local authority.

The Department of the Environment's Planning and Land Section, Custom House, Dublin 1 (tel. 01-679 3377 or www.enfo.ie) publishes a series of planning leaflets that will take your through the entire planning process.

Aside from local amenity and environmental concerns you should also check to make sure that there are no local residency restrictions (as now apply in Co. Wicklow and part of the Gaeltacht). Most of all, give yourself plenty of time to manoeuvre the planning process, to find a good architect, engineer or surveyor and a professional, recognised builder. You may find that raising the finance for your holiday home is the least of your troubles.

Selecting a builder

There is such a premium on good tradespeople in Ireland at the moment that you must be very careful about who you engage to build your holiday home. Ideally, a local firm, with plenty of experience in the area with a cast-iron reputation and references is ideal, but may not be practicable, especially if you are in any kind of a hurry. (Patience is definitely a virtue when dealing with tradespeople.)

The following checklist will help keep your project and its budget, on course:

- Decide whether you intend to project manage the site or prefer to turn it over to a professional, such as an architect, engineer, or builder. Do not undertake such a job yourself if you have no experience and insufficient time. If you do hire a professional, after checking their bonafides with the Construction Industry Federation (tel. 01-497 7487), or related organisations like Homebond (tel. 1850 306 300), thc Irish Homc Builders Association (tel. 01-406 6000) and the National Guild of Master Craftsmen (tel 01-473 2543) or the Royal Institute of Architects (tel 01-676 1803), be prepared to liase regularly with the site manager, and to familiarise yourself with every stage of the building process.

- Set a realistic budget. Speak to your lender or financial advisor before you begin the project to see how much you can afford to pay for this self-built holiday home. Then carefully research the costs and add an additional 10% contingency fund; few building projects ever come in exactly on time or on budget.

- Make sure you budget not just for the building costs but extras like stamp duty, legal fees and insurance. Factor in ongoing annual costs like utilities, maintenance, insurance and rates and charges.

- If you intend to rent your holiday home when you are in residence, research the market and then set a realistic rent and rental period. Always underestimate the contribution that the rental stream will make to your mortgage repayment schedule.
- Take plenty of time to plan and discuss the design and layout of your new holiday home with the architect or builder. It will be much more costly to reverse or alter your plans during the building process.

3

Buying holiday property abroad

Our obsession with bricks and mortar means that Ireland has one of the largest home owning populations – nearly 85% - in the entire world. We don't just buy houses, apartments, holiday homes in Ireland; we also spend billions every year investing in residential and commercial property abroad.

Clearly, our grey skies and rainy climate is a motivating factor in our passion for ocean views and golf course residences in Spain and Portugal, the two most popular purchase destinations. But in recent years, Irish people are buying property in other sunny regions of the EU, such as the south of France, Italy, Greece, Cyprus and Malta. Even non-EU countries like Turkey, Slovenia, Croatia, Bulgaria, the states of Florida and Arizona in the USA and faraway South Africa have attracted thousands of sun-seeking holiday-home buyers and retirees.

Few buyers use their holiday home for more than a few weeks, however, and many aim to pay off the mortgage by letting the property out for part or all of the year. Others buy strictly for the capital gain and tax relief which they believe justifies leaving the property unoccupied, at least until they are ready to retire or to sell it off.

Investment properties abroad have become an increasingly important asset class for qualifying personal pension investors who recognise the financial merits of adding one to their wider pension portfolio. The latest EU member states like Hungary, Poland, the Czech Republic and the Baltic countries have become the latest targets of Irish property investors for at least two of the same reasons they once targeted Spain and Portugal – low prices and cost of living compared to home.

Buying property abroad can be hugely rewarding, but it is important to keep your head and apply the same rigorous buying procedures and checks that you would if you were buying a family home or an investment property back in Ireland.

Whatever you do, don't buy a foreign property on impulse or off plans without seeing the actual property. The grass is not always greener or the skies bluer on the other side of the Irish Sea – give yourself a cooling off period before you sign any contract.

Whether you are buying in Marbella or Montreal the same checklist applies. Issues to consider include:

Location

- Is the location suitable, not just for your personal taste and interests, but for re-sale purposes?

- Is there reasonable road and transport access to the airport/train/ ferry?

- Is it in a remote and isolated area, or within reasonable access to facilities such as shops, café's and restaurants, entertainment? If it is the former, keep in mind that you might be limited to the pool of prospective buyers if you ever wish to sell. If it is in the middle of a noisy, built-up resort, you can forget about selling it to families or older people.

- Is it within reasonable reach of a good beach or beauty spot?

- Is the cost of travel to your new property secure and reasonable?

- Are you fully aware of future planning arrangements near your home?

Facilities

If you buy an investment property in a resort area, make sure the facilities are appropriate to your own needs or to the constituency you hope to attract to rent your villa or apartment, such as:

- Easy access to the beach or sea.
- Plenty of restaurants, cafes and bars/clubs.
- Amusements for young children, teenagers, older people.
- Sports facilities, such as pools/water parks, tennis and basketball courts, watersports.
- A nearby hospital or clinic.
- Good shopping areas.

If you are buying a property with an eye to retiring to it some day, and it is not in a town or village, you will want to pay special attention to public transport, access to shopping and medical centres (ideally with English-speaking medical staff if you do not speak the language), the location of the local social welfare office or department (especially if you are transferring state pension benefits) and security.

Finance

Irish lenders will not usually extend stand-alone mortgage finance for overseas properties, whether for personal use or investment purposes because of the legal difficulties in securing their interest in the event of the buyer defaulting on payments. One lender, AIB Bank does has an arrangement with a Spanish bank to assist its customers purchase apartments and villas, but you are also advised to shop around for the best value mortgage in Spain.

Irish homeowners with sufficient equity in their principal private residences can, however, take out home equity loans with their existing lender to raise a mortgage for their overseas property. Every bank applies its own lending criteria, but a 90% loan to value ratio is available plus sufficient proof that repayments can be met comfortably. Arranging an equity release mortgage could put you family home at risk if you default on the holiday home or investment property.

Historically low interest rates have made the equity release option very popular, but rates are expected to rise and you should make sure that you stress test any equity release mortgage by at least an additional 2% **before** you buy the holiday home.

For example, adding an additional €150,000 to an existing mortgage of €50,000 over 20 years will cost you c€1,100 a month at current low rates of 3%. Increase those rates to 5% and your monthly mortgage rises by €200 to c.€1,300. However, bad enough as that is, the total cost of the loan rises from €264,000 to €312,000.

Additional costs

The mortgage is just one part of this overseas property deal. You also need to engage your own solicitor at home to secure the mortgage finance and a local lawyer or *notaire* to negotiate and complete the sale in the foreign destination. You should certainly have an independent survey of the property conducted and do rigorous planning and by-law checks.

Purchase taxes and other fees can also add up and estate agents fees, which can be as high as 9% to 12% (on the sale of a property) in parts of the North America and France, also need to be budgeted into your final costings. Before you sign any final contract, you should also consider the size of local and municipal taxes every year, the cost of maintenance contracts, fitting and decoration, letting fees, and any capital gains or inheritance tax in the event of the disposal of the property.

Don't forget to also factor in the cost of traveling to and from the foreign destination (if necessary) to close the deal.

Consider hedging

Keep in mind too that exchange rate fluctuations outside the EU can have a detrimental (as well as beneficial) effect on your investment. Someone who bought a house in Florida two or three years ago, for example, is now looking at a property that is worth about 30% less because of the way the US dollar has weakened since the second half of 2004.

One way to avoid this volatility problem – at least temporarily – is to 'hedge' your transaction. The Hungarian forint presented a classic example of the need to consider hedging when in 2002 there was a growing concern about the Hungarian government's ability to manage its growing budget deficit. The forint weakened steadily through 2003 – just as many Irish investors started investing heavily in property in Budapest – until an increase in official interest rates from 6.5% to 12.5% restored some stability. By early 2004 the forint strengthened by 6% against the euro, though it remained trading at the lower end of its agreed exchange rate band of 240-280.

More recently an investor who agreed to buy an apartment in Budapest in December 2004 for 25 million forints, or €100,806 found that by his closing date of February 2005, the price of the apartment had risen to €102,627. Had the investor negotiated a foreign exchange hedging facility with his bank he could have avoided paying the additional €1,821.

Legal Issues

Many southern European countries require down-payments of as much as 30% of the property value, even before searches and surveys and the finance can be completed. In such a case you must ensure that you have a proper exit route for yourself and your down-payment if you do pull out of the deal.

Establishing the title, boundaries, etc., can often take a great deal of time in many rural areas, as can securing planning permission if you plan to make major renovations or repairs. Notaries can do much of this work, but the job of the notary is not to protect the interests of either the buyer or seller, but to see that the property is bought and sold in accordance with the law. This is why you need good, independent legal representation in the foreign country.

Residency, tax liabilities on rental income and profits if you subsequently sell your property; disputes over planning changes and inheritance are all issues that you need to be aware of as well. Just because people speak English in the USA or South Africa doesn't mean the legal system is the same as it is here or in the UK, which thankfully, is roughly similar to Ireland's. You should be especially careful about buying property in non-EU countries where language and legal traditions may be very different and red tape and corruption is unavoidable.

The inheritance tax system varies from country to country, but rules which, for example, only allow property to be inherited tax-free by offspring rather than by spouses, or where capital acquisition tax is liable even between spouses, can be circumvented in some countries by writing wills specific to this asset, and/or by registering the purchase through a limited company rather than buying it personally.

Another way to cut punitive death duties may be to buy the overseas property jointly with your adult children, or put it in their names and retain a life interest in the property. But you will need to be careful not to trigger gift tax or stamp duties.

Again, a good English-speaking solicitor is invaluable in clarifying these issues.

Taxation

If you intend to rent your overseas property, you might be well advised to hire a management company that advertises and vets the tenants, collects the rents and arranges the maintenance contracts. Be prepared to pay fees of between 10%-20% of the annual rental income for this service.

Depending on your residence status and any double taxation agreements, you may have to pay tax on this income. You should speak to a tax advisor here about your tax obligations.

Your residential investment property, whether bought at home or abroad, attracts generous tax relief. The following expenses can normally be deducted from the gross rent for tax purposes:

- interest paid on the mortgage
- rent payable on the property
- service charges
- goods provided and services rendered in connection with the letting of the property
- repairs, insurance, maintenance and management fees
- capital allowance of 12.5% per annum on the value of the fixtures and fittings
- mortgage protection premiums

You will need to declare your gross rent and expenses in your annual tax return, and pay any preliminary tax and file the return by October 31st. Make sure you keep all receipts and rental books for inspection by the Revenue Commissioners. See Chapter 4 page 84 for more.

Capital Gains Tax

Again, the tax on disposal of a property varies from country to country, but it can also depend very much on your residence status and whether there are double taxation agreements between Ireland and other countries. Capital Gains Tax here is just 20% on second properties that are not your private principal residence, but this rate can be much higher in other jurisdictions, especially if you dispose of the property before a certain number of years has elapsed, or if you are a non-resident.

Your Irish tax-advisor should be consulted to suggest the best disposal formula for your circumstances.

The most popular countries for overseas property investment by Irish buyers are Spain, Portugal, the United Kingdom, France and the United States.

Spain

Spain is a favourite destination of Irish property buyers, but prices have soared in recent years and real bargains are not as easy to find. The legal and tax systems are quite different and you must ensure that you have an independent, English-speaking lawyer working strictly on your behalf, both in Spain and here in Ireland to complete the deal. Consider the following checklist:

- Undertake your inspection trip independently and not with a property promotion group.
- Visit prospective properties in winter and summer.
- Be aware that you have just seven days to pay the minimum 10% deposit once you have signed the contract. The deposit is transferable, but not refundable if you pull out of the deal.
- Notary fees are charged at flat rates of between €300 and €1,200.
- Transfer taxes amount to 6% - 7% of the purchase price, but you should put aside 3% of the purchase price to cover your legal, registration fees, etc. Purchases of new properties directly from the developer are charged at a 7% IVA (the equivalent of VAT) plus 0.5%-1% stamp duty depending on location.
- If you are dealing with a builder, make sure he is properly licensed.
- Time-share deals now include a 14 day cooling off period, but this fortnight's grace does not apply if you buy directly from a developer.

- Ask about planning developments in the area and be aware that some Spanish local authorities allow developers to charge existing residents the cost of installing new roads or amenities like water filtration or sewerage treatment works.

- Make sure the last owner has not used his property as collateral for other debts; you could be liable.

- Residents and non-residents are subject to a flat rate of 25% on rental income as well as a wealth tax, for which a complicated formula applies.

- Spanish capital gains tax of 35% for non-residents, and inheritance tax can be reduced or avoided by setting up a Spanish company to buy the property. The CGT reduces to 20% instead of 35% in such a case.

- Five percent of the gross sale value is automatically set aside for tax purposes, and if the CGT is greater than 5% you will owe the Spanish authorities the balance within 30 days of the sale. If it is less, you will be entitled to a refund that can take 90 days or longer to receive. An 'adjusted purchase price', which takes into account inflation indexing can reduce this bill.

- If you buy buildings and contents insurance for your Spanish property make sure the policy is valid under Spanish law first. Such a policy is likely to be more expensive than a Spanish one. All-risks policies that provide world-wide cover for your contents are not always available from Spanish insurers.

Portugal

The tax laws regarding property have been recently amended with positive consequences for Irish investors:

- The cost of buying new property in Portugal can be high, with a standard value added tax (IVA) of 19% on the purchase price of new homes (which should be included in the purchase price). IMT or transfer tax (the equivalent of our stamp duty) is payable on second-hand properties and ranges from 2% to 8% on values of €80,000 up to €500,000 plus.

Off-shore domiciled buyers, who purchase via a company, must now pay a flat 15% IMT.

- Notaries fees are usually fixed at 2.5% of the sale price. Legal fees usually amount to another 1%-2% of the purchase price. Hiring a lawyer to close your sale is optional in Portugal, but is recommended.

- Property searches and surveys of second hand properties can take an inordinately long period of time in rural Portugal and you need to ensure that you always take independent legal advice, preferably with an English-speaking lawyer.

- Property tax is based on the rateable value of the property by its local authority, but if your property is owned by an offshore company it is liable to a fixed rate tax of 2%, which may be higher than the standard property tax if you were simply a non-resident owner. However, if you have paid IMT, and are a Portugese resident, you may qualify for a property tax exemption for up to 10 years.

- Capital gains tax does not apply to non-residents and inheritance tax has been abolished, though in some cases there may be a 10% transfer tax on gifts.

- The law of 'subrogation' applies in Portugal, meaning that all property debts – including mortgages, local taxes and community charges - remain with the property and are inherited by the new owner. Before you complete the purchase you must ensure that the property is free of all debts and liens.

- Cover for earthquakes, lightning damage and subsidence are not usually included in Portugese buildings insurance policies; be sure to check all exclusions carefully. Check to see if you can insure your property legally with an Irish company instead.

The United Kingdom

Luckily for Irish property investors, the system for buying and selling property in the UK is nearly identical with our system, with the same process of title searches, the registration of deeds, the use of a solicitor for conveyancing. A double taxation agreement is also in place, the language and weather is the same and the legal system is familiar. And while tax and stamp duty rates – for income tax, CGT and inheritance are quite different, unless you are a UK resident for tax purposes, most are not particularly relevant. UK stamp duty is lower than in Ireland.

But the rates were recently been amended in the 2005 Budget and properties worth between £250,000 and £500,000 are now charged stamp duty at 3% instead of 1%, though the tax exempt threshold has been raised from £60,000 to £120,000.

Your Irish solicitor may be able to recommend a UK colleague to handle the purchase, title search and property registration. Your mortgage advisor and solicitor here can handle the mortgage arrangements if you raise finance on an equity release basis.

Rental income repatriated from the UK to Ireland is subject to Irish income tax rules. There is no Capital Gains Tax liability on UK investments held by non-residents and UK property held by an Irish resident will not be subject to UK inheritance tax if the benefit is remitted to Irish beneficiaries.

The biggest risk you take in buying UK property – aside from the usual market rent and capital fluctuations - is the potential volatility in the value of sterling and the euro and the ongoing cost of foreign exchange transactions.

The average cost of a house in Britain was £172,788 in 2004, up from £77,531 in 1997, but house price rises have slowed down considerably over the past year due to a number of interest rate hikes.

France

French property tax rules were amended at the beginning of 2004, reducing, for example, capital gains tax on the sale of property by EU residents who are not resident in France to a flat rate of 16%. However, the cost of buying property in France can be very high, the system is extremely bureaucratic and formal and renting out your property in France can be extremely problematic as tenants have very strong residency rights.

- Always use a lawyer and notaire who speaks good English. Remember that the notaire acts for both parties and may charge up to 3% of the buying price. The lawyer will charge another 1%-2%.

- Transfer tax (the equivalent of stamp duty) is 7.5% but less than 1% on new properties.

- Once your deposit is paid – typically 10% of the asking price - the deal is binding.

- You are not obliged to buy through an estate agent, though most foreign buyers do so. Fees can typically amount to 7%-8% of the purchase price, though they can sometimes be split between the buyer and seller.

- Tenants are well protected by French law so make sure your lawyer explains your obligations and rights if you buy an apartment which you intend to rent out on a long term basis.

- Inquire about the French government 'Leaseback Scheme' which allows you to lease your property to a holiday company that guarantees you an annual rental income of between 3%-6% for up to nine years or longer. This company is responsible for upkeep and maintenance (but not annual property taxes) and must return your property to you at the agreed maturity date in pristine order. The advantage of the scheme is VAT exemption (of 19.6%) on new properties or villas; you are still allowed to occupy the property for certain weeks of the year at no cost. The early sale of the property is permitted but you will be obliged to refund a proportion of the exempted VAT.

- Non-resident property owners should write a French will to deal exclusively with your property there, and your Irish will should exclude references to the French property. Inheritance tax is not exempt between spouses in France though double taxation agreements do apply between Ireland and France.
- Capital gains tax for non-resident property owners is now a flat 16% but subject to certain conditions, you are exempt if you are the holder of an old age pension or you are an invalid.

Florida, USA

Irish holiday home buyers and investors are increasingly attracted to properties in the United States, especially in southern states like Arizona and Florida. This is not just because of the fine weather, but because buying and selling costs, and tax rates are very low compared to Ireland and Europe:

- It is not necessary to use a lawyer to complete a property transaction. Instead 'title companies' are used which charge quite low fees in the region of $150 to $300 dollars. You can hire a lawyer to represent your interest who will also charge a flat fee, perhaps as little as $500-$600. You will need to buy 'title insurance' however, which protects you if there is problem with the ownership rights of the property you are buying. This usually costs about 1% of the cost of purchase price.
- Instead of a sales tax on property, there are 'closing' costs which include Documentary Stamps of 35 cents in every $100 dollars of a mortgage and Intangible Tax at a rate of 0.002% of any mortgage you take out in Florida. However, if you pay cash for your Florida home (from a mortgage raised on your existing property in Ireland) these taxes do not apply. Annual property taxes are paid to the local county authority and are usually based on 75% of your property's market value with a percentage tax rate of usually no more than 1.5%-2% of that discounted valuation.

- Rental income is taxable, but generous tax allowances on property substantially reduce any liability and double taxation agreements exist between the US and Ireland.
- If you sell your Florida property, estate agents will charge up to 6% of the sale price and Documentary Stamps on the deed will be charged at a rate of 70 cents on every $100 dollars of value. This will amount to a $700 charge on a property worth $100,000.
- Capital gains tax is only applied on sales profits in excess of $250,000 per owner; a married couple could earn $500,000 from the sale of their property before paying any tax. Although depending on your residence status you may have to pay CGT in Ireland.
- There is no inheritance tax on estates worth less than $1.5 million dollars.
- It is absolutely essential to have comprehensive health insurance if you visit or live in Florida; private hospital treatment is extremely expensive.
- Getting buildings and contents insurance is problematic in Florida where hurricane damage and flooding is commonplace in coastal areas. Consult a good insurance broker in Florida and/or in Ireland about the cost and availability of cover. This could effect your ability to secure an Irish mortgage.

When France is the place for you...

The South of France has been the playground of the rich and famous, of royalty and artists for nearly 200 years and now it is within the scope of many ordinary Irish investors.

But perhaps you don't just fancy a retreat in Antibes? How about an apartment in the Alps, a mountain getaway in the Ardeche or a summer house on the Brittany coast? Under the French 'Leaseback' holiday property investment scheme, you can buy a property for a mere €100,000 or for more than €1,000,000. Ultimately, it could cost you very little indeed.

Set up by the French government over 20 years ago to encourage the building of quality holiday rental properties in both established and newly identified resort areas; the Irish are now top of the list of buyers of leaseback properties which guarantee annual rental return of between 3%-6% for lease periods of up to eleven years and a 19.6% VAT refund over a 20 year period.

All costs and charges are covered by the lease contract, including the fitting out and decorating of the property. And while owners can have up to six week's access to the property for their own use, this will result in a sharp reduction in the agreed annual return. But because the property is owned by the individual investor and not the management company, it is always yours to sell, though this will result in a clawback of a portion of the VAT refund.

Choosing a leaseback should follow the same criteria as any other holiday or buy-to-let property: location is the key and you want to ensure that your leaseback scheme is located in a popular tourist area, has good road access and is well designed and equipped with the kind of amenities that appeal to both individuals and families. Crucially, check what airport or ferry services are nearby and if there are frequent flights from Ireland. Consider its potential resale value by researching other mature properties in the area; it is worth also speculating as to whether this property will always only be a holiday purchase, or a full-time residential home for someone.

Leaseback schemes are designed to take much of the hassle out of owning an investment property in France, but that doesn't mean that you should drop your guard. You still need good, independent legal and tax advice from an English speaking advisor. You will be given all the documents – in English – from the property promoter, many of which now use Irish estate agents as their go-between – but you should not assume this will be a direct translation.

Fighting your corner, however, is the Notaire. In France the notary fulfills the same role as your conveyance solicitor here. Their fee – usually about €1,000 - is paid up front with your deposit. Once you are satisfied that you understand the contract, and the detailed specifications of the property, you will need to sign every page of the contract.

The following checklist can help you decide whether a leaseback is the right way to buy a holiday investment home in France (or Spain and Portugal, two other destinations where such properties are also available).

- Check the size carefully: A studio size apartment may be perfect for most holiday makers, but will it be suitable if you have a family? Would a one or two bedroom property have a better resale value than a studio?

- Is this property entirely for investment purposes or are you considering retiring there someday? Wear both hats when determining if it is a suitable property.

- Are you willing and able to tie up your money for 9-11 years?

- The annual return will be adjusted according to inflation, but will not take into account interest rate rises you may face. Is an average 3%-6% yield (indexed to inflation) sufficient to meet your borrowing costs?

- Establish from the outset how your return will be paid – quarterly or annually.

- Find out if car parking space is included in the price or is extra. Expect to pay up to 10% extra for such a space.

- Set out exactly the impact that using the property yourself will have on your annual return.

- You may be required to pay a portion of the selling price in stages, depending on whether your leaseback scheme is already built or under construction. Ask for a clear payment schedule.

- Find out which taxes will be paid by the management company and which tax you are obliged to pay yourself.

Leaseback arrangements are not for everybody. You may get better value from your investment, and have easier access to your money and property if you are willing to investigate the market yourself and hire an independent management company. Before you choose either option make sure you thoroughly investigate both.

4

Buying an investment property

Buying an investment property is the Irish property market these days. This is where you start on the road to becoming a property millionaire, or simply having some extra cash when you retire.

It is not a fail safe investment method. There are no guarantees that you will make money from your capital. But it is a relatively safe bet. Remember those words of advice from your father about land – they ain't making it anymore. It's truer now than when you first heard that old saying.

But let's get one thing straight from the start: you can no longer become a property millionaire overnight in Ireland. Many people did in the 1990s when chronically undervalued property, that nobody wanted and nobody could afford, based in a struggling economy, created an investor's paradise.

That's no reason to moan about the fact that you could have bought a semi-detached house in 1990 for €50,000 and sold it for €300,000 five years later. If you were one of the lucky ones, well done. If you are coming into the market now, despite high prices beginning to plateau, you still have some advantages the investor back in 1990 did not have.

First, that investor found it very difficult to get finance. Banks were not as generous with mortgages back then as they are now. Crucifying mortgage rates and low wages made it just as difficult in 1990 to buy a house as it is now. In the middle of the upward cycle for property, there was the currency crisis of 1993 when the old Irish pound was devalued and mortgage interest rates hit a high of 17%. But, yes, had you been able to ride out that storm with just two reasonably situated semis, you could be a millionaire today.

You can still become wealthy by investing in Irish property, but maybe not as quickly. What you need to look at now are the exciting opportunities handed to you by a buoyant economy and a Europe with no frontiers.

The typical Irish property buyer now earns more income than at any previous time, and is sitting on valuable property in an upward moving European country with a stable economy. Your wages are higher, and the equity you have built up in whatever property you own is far higher than it was ten years ago.

Added to this is the fact that lending institutions are more competitive. The days of mortgage waiting lists and interviews with the bank manager are over and the banks are very comfortable lending to investors due to the Irish property boom. With Irish people buying investment property in every Irish county and all over Europe and the US, the banks are familiar with their customer's needs, and what they can and cannot offer.

Is there a new Euro-Tiger?

With Irish prices high, but yields on residential investments tight, focus has shifted to the UK and Europe; but be careful when reading wildly optimistic stories about countries being touted as the next Euro-Tiger. Dirt cheap apartments in some European cities may well still be dirt cheap in 20 years time.

Ireland's property boom has been quite unique, fuelled by a rapid rise in demand, rapid job growth, which was created in turn by radical tax changes and significant inward investment. The pressure for housing really started to build when our own emigrants started returning in their tens of thousands in the mid-90s and now there is huge influx of immigrants from the new EU member states of the east and north.

All of these house hunters have bought scarce housing stock, and have driven up prices. The same set of circumstance cannot be said of many other countries where investment properties are on offer at a fraction of the price here. In much of Europe there is not the same unique desire that we have to buy and own a home; people are quite happy to rent for most of their lives so there is no massive surge of first time homeowners always looking for property. Ageing populations also limit the buying pool.

This isn't to say that there are no good buying opportunities in every European country – there clearly has been a surge of ownership and values in Spain, Portugal and France and in certain cities and locations in the emerging EU countries, though whether this is mainly due to overseas investors or strong indigenous demand is debatable.

There are no property price guarantees, but what is certain is that you must know exactly what you are getting into whether you invest here at home or abroad.

Where to buy

If you intend to buy and then rent your property, it needs to be where people want to live. But it also needs to be in a place where, ideally, there is a large pool of tenants who, much as they would love to own a property themselves in this desirable location, are simply not in such a position. Recognising supply trends is the one of the keys to successful property investing.

Another market for your rental property of course are the people who are not interested in buying. Executives on temporary postings and other overseas workers who only intend to remain here for a few years are also a good source of tenant: For them, high sales costs and mortgages are pointless, but they do require good quality accommodation close to the companies and service industries that employ them.

Buying investment property in a location far from a town or larger urban center can be risky. Transport might be a big issue for lower paid workers especially and the location of your property is major bus or train routes and motorways will also make all the difference to it being fully let or lying idle.

One of the most important factors about location is the historic performance of property in that locality: if houses and apartments are always in demand in that neighbourhood, town or city, your property should perform well. Keep in mind too that an area that doesn't rent well is probably also going to be a hard sell. The entire purpose of a buy-to-let property is to make money, and have someone else pay the mortgage.

Stamp Duty

If you purchase a property for investment purposes Stamp Duty will be payable as follows:

Market Value	Houses/Apartments
Up to €127,000	Nil
€127,001 - €190,500	3.00%
€190,501 - €254,000	4.00%
€254,001 - €317,500	5.00%
€317,501 - €381,000	6.00%
€381,001 - €635,000	7.00%
Over €635,000	9.00%

The rate of Stamp Duty on a non-residential property is as follows:

Market Value	Non Residential Properties
Up to €10,000	Exempt
€10,001 - €20,000	1%
€20,001 - €30,000	2%
€30,001 - €40,000	3%
€40,001 - €70,000	4%
€70,001 - €80,000	5%
€80,001 - €100,000	6%
€100,001 - €120,000	7%
€120,001 - €150,000	8%
Over €150,000	9%

You may be able to include the Stamp Duty as part of your mortgage, but it is a significant cost that must be factored in early in your plans.

Legal issues

If you are buying as part of a partnership or with friends, it is vitally important that you all approach it as a business. Remember that friendships can fall through, turning things very messy. From the very start you must all establish, and agree exactly, how much each individual has invested and their exact stake in the property. This is vital as the property increases in value. It is important that each partners' share of the growth is proportionate to their original stake.

Since property is not as liquid an asset as shares, there must also be careful consideration to the type of exit strategy that will be in place should the partnership break down, and this includes how the property will be divided up by the consortium in the event of the sale of the property.

Another consideration is how to deal with one or more people wanting to liquidate their share: should the others be required to automatically buy them out, or should there be a specific time-frame agreed by the consortium so that profit-taking is not done say, without proper notice? For example, it is not uncommon in property partnerships for the parties to agree that there will be no sale for at least three years after purchase in order for purchase costs to be absorbed. Even at the end of the three year period, it is not uncommon for there to be an additional six month 'moratorium' in order to allow the other partners to raise the buy-out capital.

It is also important that this shareholding is included in the partner's wills. A solicitor will provide independent, professional advice on the best course of action so that all parties entering into such an agreement know exactly where they stand from the very beginning. Once this is done you can all engage in the business of property investment with minimal outlay by the individual. It is a very cost effective way of getting into the property game and making profits.

Property investing and tax

Property investment can give rise to two taxes - income tax on the rental income Capital Gains Tax (CGT) on investment profits.

Income tax

Rents are taxed under Schedule D Case V on the basis of the actual year's income - e.g. rents arising in the year ending 31st December 2005 are assessed to tax in the income tax year 2005. Expenses can be deducted from the gross rental income provided they are wholly and exclusively for business purposes and are not of a capital nature.

The following are examples of the type of expenses that may be claimed for:

- Rents payable by the landlord in respect of the property, i.e., ground rent.

- Service charges or levies payable on the property, i.e., water rates, refuse collection etc.
- Cost of any service or goods provided by the landlord, i.e., gas, electricity, telephone rental, cable television etc. for which they do not receive a payment from the tenant.
- Maintenance, i.e., cleaning and general servicing of the premises
- Insurance of the premises against fire.
- Management, i.e., actual cost of collection of rents, advertising, etc.
- Legal fees to cover the drawing up of leases or the issue of solicitors letters to tenants who default on payment of rent.
- Accountancy fees incurred for the purposes of preparing a rental income account.
- Wear and Tear on furniture and fittings, i.e., carpets, cookers, central heating etc.
- Interest on money borrowed for the purchase, improvement or repair of the property.
- Repairs, i.e., decorating and general upkeep of the property, landlords may not claim the cost of their own labour. Examples of common repairs which would normally be deductible in computing rental profits include:
    - exterior and interior painting and decorating
    - damp and rot treatment
    - mending broken windows, doors, furniture and machines replacing roof slates.

- Mortgage protection policy premiums with effect from 1st January 2002.

Wear and tear

If you let a property which is furnished you can claim for a wear and tear allowance based on the cost of the furniture and fittings. It will be necessary to retain an itemised list of expenditure incurred each year.

- From 4th December 2002 the rate of wear and tear is 12.5% per year over eight years.
- For the period between 1st December 2001 and 3rd December 2002 the rate was 20% per year over five years.
- Prior to 1st January 2001 the rate was 15% per year for the first six years and 10% in the seventh year.

Non allowable expenses

- Expenses which have been incurred before the property was let also known as pre-letting expenses. The exception to this rule are auctioneers letting fees, advertising fees and legal fees incurred on the first letting.
- Expense incurred between lettings are allowed for tax purposes provided the landlord didn't occupy the property during the period and a new lease is granted.
- Expenses incurred after the property has been let for the last time, i.e. post letting expenses are not allowed.
- Capital expenditure on additions alterations or improvement to the premises, unless they are specifically allowed under a tax incentive scheme (see chapter 5 page 111).
- If a property is let on an uneconomic basis the expenses are not allowed.
- If you repair and maintain the property yourself the cost of your own labour is not allowed.

- Interest arising on or after the 6th February 2003 on a loan which was used to purchase the rental property from a spouse. This restriction does not apply in the case of a legal separation or divorce.

How is profit/loss rent calculated?

The rental profit or loss is calculated by reference to the rent or total receipts to which the person becomes entitled to in any tax year (as opposed to the period to which the income relates).

> Mr. White began leasing a house from Mr. Brown on 1st December 2003. Mr. White pays rent of €2,000 in four annual installments on the first day of each quarter. He paid €2,000 on 1st December 2003. His landlord Mr. Brown became entitled to receive the quarters' rent on that date, therefore the entire €2,000 is taxable income for 2003. It is important to note that the €2,000 is not apportioned as to make two thirds of it taxable in the tax year 2004.

A typical rental income and expenditure account is shown on page 84.

Rent a Room Scheme

Where a room or rooms in a person's principal private residence is let as residential accommodation, gross annual rent of up to €7,620 will be exempt form income tax. Rental income from this scheme will not trigger a clawback of any Stamp Duty relief claimed, CGT relief on your principal private residence when you sell, mortgage interest relief or non-contributory pension benefits if you live alone.

Residential Property
Rental Income and Expenditure Account Y/E 31st December 2005

Name: ____________________ PPS No: ______________

Y/E: ______________

		€
	Rents Received	€15,000
Less:	Allowable expenses	
	Ground rents payable	€ 100
	Insurance on premises	€ 500
	Repairs and renewals	€ 900
	Light, heat and telephone	€ 400
	Cleaning and maintenance	€ 1,000
	Agency and Advertising	€ 700
	Interest on Borrowed Money	€ 6,500
	Mortgage Protection Premiums	€ 300
	Sundry Expenses	€ 300
	Total Expenses	€10,700
	Net Rental Income	€ 4,300
Less:	Capital Allowances on Fixtures & Fittings €7,000 @ 12.5%	(€ 875)
	Taxable Rental Income / After Capital Allowances	€ 3,425
	Income Tax & Levies - assuming a 42% rate of tax + 5% PRSI & Levies.	**€ 1,610**

What if a premises is only partly let?

If only part of a premises is let, only expenses incurred on that part of the premises are available for set off against rental income. For example, if rooms are let in a private house and the income received exceeds the limits of the "Rent a Room" relief, the expenses for gas, electricity, etc., are shared by all the occupants of the house, expenses applicable to that part of the house which is let are only available for set off against profit rent. Expenses should be apportioned based on the occupancy of the house, i.e., the number of rooms occupied by tenants.

A separate rental computation must be prepared for each rental property whereby the rental expenses for each property are deducted from the related rental income for the same property in order to arrive at a surplus (i.e. income greater than expenses) or a deficiency (i.e. expenses greater than income) for each property. The total of surpluses and deficiencies are then aggregated to arrive at profits or gains arising in the year, i.e. taxable rent.

What if a loss is made?

A loss will arise if total allowable expenses are more than the rents received. This loss can be set against any other profit rent made by the landlord or carried forward against future rental profits. Such losses cannot be carried back or used to shelter non-rental income.

Keeping records

You must keep full and accurate records of your lettings from the start. You need to do this whether you send in a simple summary of your profit/loss, prepare the accounts yourself, or, have an accountant do it. All supporting records such as invoices, bank and building society statements, cheque stubs, receipts etc., should also be retained. You must keep your records for six years unless your Revenue office advises you otherwise.

What if rents are payable to a non-resident landlord?

If a landlord resides outside the country and rent is paid directly to him/her or to his/her bank account either in the State or abroad, tax must be deducted by the tenant at the standard rate of tax (currently 20%) from the gross rents payable. Failure to deduct tax leaves the tenant liable for the tax that should have been deducted. The tenant must also give a Form 185 to the landlord to show that the tax has been accounted for to Revenue.

Where an agent, resident in the State, is appointed by the non-resident landlord to manage the property and the agent is collecting the rents, the rents must be paid gross to the agent. The agent is then chargeable to tax on the rents as Collection Agent for the landlord and is required to submit an annual tax return and account for the tax due under Self Assessment.

Note: The agent appointed need not be a professional person, i.e., it can be a family member or other person prepared to take on the responsibility and undertakes to make annual tax returns and account to Revenue for the tax due.

How are non-resident landlords taxed?

On receipt of the annual tax return, profit rent, i.e., rent received less allowable expenses, will be assessed. The landlord is entitled to claim relief for expenses, which are usually allowed in arriving at the rental profit. The landlord is also entitled to a credit for the tax deducted by the tenant. Form 185 should be submitted by the landlord with the tax return to obtain credit for the tax retained.

How are foreign rents taxed?

In general, income from foreign property is computed on the full amount of the income arising, irrespective of whether the income has or will be received in the State. In the case of foreign rental income this income is charged under Case III of Schedule D and the same deductions and allowances are available as if the income had been received in the State. Deductions are also normally available in respect of such income for sums in respect of foreign tax paid. This income should be included in an individual's tax return on the Foreign Income panel.

These rules do not apply to a person who is not domiciled in the State or who is an Irish citizen not ordinarily resident in the State. In such cases, income tax is computed on the full amount of the actual sums received in the State from such remittances, etc. without any deduction or relief given.

Rent allowance

Tax relief may be claimed by a tenant paying rent to a landlord for private accommodation. In order to claim this relief the tenant must complete a Form Rent 1, which is available at your local tax office. The annual tax credit allowable, in 2005, is €300 for a single person and €508 for a married couple or widowed person. If you are over 55 years the tax credit is €508 for a single person or €1,016 for a married couple or widowed person.

How do I register for Income Tax

When you buy an investment property and are not already self employed it is necessary for you to register for income tax with your Inspector of Taxes.

In order to register for income tax it is necessary for you to complete a TR1 form. This form is available from your local tax office, You can also download this form on the Revenue Commissioners web site at www.revenue.ie. The TR1 can also be used to register for VAT if required.

Capital Gains Tax

Where a property that has been let is disposed of, Capital Gains Tax may arise on the disposal. The chargeable gain is calculated by deducting any allowable expenditure from the amount realised on the disposal.

The allowable expenditure may include:

- The cost of acquisition of the property and any costs of acquisition such as solicitors/auctioneers fees.
- Any costs incurred in improving the value of the property.
- Any costs of disposal such as solicitors/auctioneers fees.

Expenditure on costs of acquisition and improvement may be adjusted to take account of inflation. Where a disposal is made on or after 1st January 2003, the indexation relief will only apply for the period of ownership of the asset up to 31st December 2002. No relief is due if period of ownership is less than 12 months.

VAT

Rents from short term letting of property, i.e. less than 10 years, are exempt from VAT. However, it is possible to waive this exemption and charge VAT at 21% on the rental income received. By doing this you may be entitled to claim a refund on the VAT paid on the purchase of the property. You would then be liable to VAT on your rental income received from your short term lettings. If you do waive your exemption you would then have to charge VAT on all the income you received from short term lettings. It is not possible for landlords to waive this exemption in respect of one property while not waiving the exemption on another, except in very limited circumstances.

You can cancel the waiver at any time. However if you do this you must refund to the Revenue Commissioners any excess of VAT repaid by them to you over the VAT you have collected on the rental income received.

VAT is a very complex area so it is important that you take professional advice in relation to property transactions and VAT.

Landlord legal obligations

As a landlord you have certain legal obligations (as does your tenant) under the 2004 Residential Tenancies Act. Under the Act you not only have to be registered with the Revenue Commissioners and provide your tenant with a rent book or a written lease, and 28 days notice to quit, your property also has to meet certain minimum standards and provide security of tenancy once the tenant is in residence for more than six months. Rent can only be reviewed once a year unless there have been such changes or improvements during the year to merit another review.

Residential Tenancies Board

From the 1st September 2004 it is also necessary for landlords to register their properties with the Residential Tenancies Board.

One of the major changes introduced on the 1st of September 2004 is the concept of the tenant gaining the right to remain in occupation after a six-month probationary period. After the initial six months, the tenant may remain in occupation for a period up to three and a half years. The tenancy becomes known as a Part 4 Tenancy. The landlord may terminate the tenancy during this period on specified grounds only and these are outlined below.

Terminating a Tenancy

If a tenancy is terminated within the first six months, not due to any fault on the tenant and there is no fixed-term lease, the landlord must serve notice to quit of at least 28 days. The landlord does not have to provide a reason for terminating the tenancy.

Landlord terminating a Part 4 tenancy

The notice period required to terminate a Part 4 tenancy is regulated by the length of the tenancy.

Notice Period	Duration of Tenancy
28 days	Less than 6 months
35 days	6 months or more but less than 1 year
42 days	1 year or more but less than 2 years
56 days	2 years or more but less than 3 years
84 days	3 years or more but less than 4 years
112 days	4 or more years

The landlord must provide a reason for terminating the tenancy.

A landlord may terminate a Part 4 tenancy but only on the following grounds:

- Where the tenant has not complied with their obligations, the tenant has been notified of the breach and has not righted the breach.
- Where the dwelling is no longer suitable to the needs of the tenant.
- Where the landlord is selling the property.
- Where the landlord requires the dwelling for his own occupation or for a member of his family to occupy.
- Where the landlord intends to substantially refurbish or renovate the dwelling and planning permission has been obtained, if necessary.
- Where the landlord intends to change the use of the dwelling and planning permission has been obtained, if necessary.

The landlord may terminate a Part 4 tenancy with 7 days notice on the grounds of the tenants' anti-social behaviour. The landlord may terminate with 28 days notice where the tenant is in default. If the default is non-payment of rent, the landlord must notify the tenant in writing that the rent is owing and give them 14 days to pay the rent prior to serving 28 days notice to quit.

A tenant surrendering a tenancy must serve their landlord with the relevant notice period.

Notice Period	Duration of Tenancy
28 days	Less than 6 months
35 days	6 months or more but less than 1 year
42 days	1 year or more but less than 2 years
56 days	2 years or more but less than 3 years
56 days	3 years or more but less than 4 years
56 days	4 or more years

Registration

The majority of tenancies will have to be registered with the Private Residential Tenancies Board. It is the responsibility of the landlord to register the details with the Board. Either the landlord or the tenants are entitled to a copy of the details entered on the register.

All tenancies must be registered with the Private Residential Tenancies Board (PRTB). All new tenancies must be registered within one month of the commencement of the tenancy.

The following details must be supplied with the registration application

- The address of the dwelling .
- The name, address and PPS number of the landlord and any authorised agents.
- The number of occupants of the dwelling.
- The name and PPS number(if known) of the tenants, or tenants.
- A description of the dwelling including the number of bed spaces.
- The date the tenancy commenced.
- The amount of rent payable.

The fee payable to register a tenancy is €70. If a landlord is registering a number of tenancies in a single dwelling, the fee is €300.

Private Residential Tenancies Board

The Private Residential Tenancies Board (PRTB) has been set up to resolve disputes between Landlord and Tenants, to operate a system of tenancy registration and provide information and policy advice. Landlords and tenants may refer disputes to the Private Residential Tenancies Board for resolution by mediation, a judication or tribunal hearing.

The Board deals with:

- The refund or retention of deposits.
- Alleged breaches of tenancy obligations, by either Landlords or Tenants.
- Timing of rent reviews and the determination of rent levels following a review.
- Failure to follow the correct procedure to terminate a tenancy.
- Invalid reason for terminating a tenancy.
- Determining proper notice periods.
- Tenants vacating tenancies in the absence of a valid notice.
- Tenants and sub-tenants remaining in occupation despite the receipt of a valid notice.
- Claims for costs and damages from either the landlord or the tenant arising from failures to comply with their obligations.
- Claims for costs or damages or both by a landlord or tenant alleging improper termination of a tenancy.
- Failure to comply with a determination order made by the Board.
- Penalisation of tenants by landlords.
- Claims for rent arrears or other charges.

Market Rent

Landlords are restricted from charging rent that is above the market rate. After the first twelve months of a tenancy, landlords can seek a rent review. Reviews cannot take place more frequently than annually unless there has been a substantial change in the nature of the accommodation during that period.

For more details you should contact the Private Residential Tenancies Board, Tel. 01 888 2960 Canal House, Canal Road, Ranelagh, Dublin 6.

Commercial property

The value of commercial property is normally directly related to the rental income it can generate. In the table below, we highlight how rental income from commercial properties has been increasing at different paces over the years. This illustration* outlines the average cost per square foot of commercial properties in the Dublin area over the past 30 years.

Year	Average office rental cost per sq. ft. €	Average retail rental cost per sq. ft. (shopping centres) €	Average industrial rental cost per sq. ft. €
1975	€4.50	n/a	n/a
1985	€12.00	€24.00	€3.20
1995	€16.50	€160.00	€8.50
2005	€45.00	€260.00	€12.00

(* Source: Insignia Richard Ellis Gunne Research)

When it comes to investing in property it is always wise not to lose sight of both the current and long-term potential return on your investment.

Rental Properties

Individuals who purchase rental properties normally have substantial incomes, so the rate of tax on rental income will generally be high (42% tax plus 5% PRSI & levies).

The rate of Corporation Tax on rental income is 25%. Undistributed rental income in a closed company is liable to a surcharge of 20% so the effective Corporation Tax rate can be as high as 40%.

Tax on disposal

When a property is sold the taxable proceeds will normally be subject to CGT at 20%, so, if you own the property personally you retain proceeds, less 20% CGT. If the property is owned by a company it also pays CGT at 20%. However, there will be a further personal tax liability if you wish to gain access to the cash within the company. If you access the cash by way of salary or dividend, the rate could be as high as 42%. The other option is to liquidate the company, though this will give rise to a new 20% CGT liability or what is commonly known as the double "hit".

Marie set up her company, Acme Ltd. with ordinary share capital of €2. Acme Ltd. bought a property for letting for €130,000. Acme Ltd later sold the building for €500,000. Here we assume indexation of 30% for CGT purposes and that the company has no other assets or liabilities.

The tax position for Marie is also illustrated as if she bought the property personally.		
	Personal purchase €	Acme Limited €
Sale Proceeds	€500,000	€500,000
Less: Cost of property plus indexation	€130,000	€130,000
Taxable Amount	€370,000	€370,000
CGT on €370,000 @ 20%	€74,000	€74,000
Available for distribution		€426,000
CGT on liquidation of A Limited €426,000 @ 20%		€85,200
Net personal proceeds	€426,000	€340,800
Total Tax payable	**€74,000**	**€159,200**

Tax liability on sale of investment property

In August 2004, a married couple, Aidan and Rachel, sold an investment property, a three bedroom house, for €300,000. Sales costs amounted to €5,000. They had bought the house in August 1972 for €30,000. The market value of the house at 6th April 1974 was €32,000. The couple had added an extension costing €20,000 to the house in March 1988. The house was not their principal residence and they had no other chargeable gains in the tax year 2004.

Capital gain computation 2004

		€	
	Sales Price		€300,000
Less:	Selling Costs		€5,000
Deduct:			€295,000
	Value on 6th April 1974 adjusted for inflation: i.e. €32,000 x 7.528	€240,896	
	1987/88 Expenditure, adjusted for inflation: i.e. €20,000 x 1.583	€31,660	€272,556
	Capital Gain		€22,444
Less:	Exemption (House in Joint Name)		€2,540
	Taxable @ 20%		€19,904
	Tax Payable		**€3,981**

Note: The Capital Gains Tax of €3,981 will be payable on 31st October 2004.

Renting while abroad

Many homeowners going abroad to work or travel for a limited period will rent their home while they are away, especially now that the cost of re-entering the Irish property market is so high. In fact, so much equity is now built into established owners' Irish property that they often use it to purchase a property – rather than rent – in their foreign posting. If you do rent your home while you are away, this income is taxable in Ireland regardless of residence status.

The following is an example of how the tax liability can fall due if you rent your home while abroad:

The rent is €1,000 a month or €12,000 per annum. The outstanding mortgage is €85,000, with annual mortgage interest payments of €4,800 and outgoings (agency fees, insurance, repairs etc.) of €1,600.		
		€
	Gross Rental Income	€12,000
Less:	Mortgage Interest	(€4,800)
	Outgoings	(€1,600)
	Taxable Income	**€5,600** @ 20% or 42%

Capital Gains Tax (CGT)

When you sell your main private residence it is normally exempt from CGT. However, if you have rented your main private residence for a number of years, at the date of sale, the CGT exemption will be restricted on a time basis.

For CGT purposes, certain periods of absence are regarded as periods of occupation e.g.

- The last 12 months of ownership.
- Any period of absence throughout which you worked in a foreign employment or any period of absence not exceeding four years during which you were prevented from occupying the residence because of employment, provided you occupy the residence before and after the period of absence.

Capital gains tax indexation factors

Year of purchase	Year of Disposal							
	97/98	98/99	99/00	00/01	2001	2002	2003	2004
1974/75	6.112	6.215	6.313	6.582	6.930	7.180	7.528	7.528
1975/76	4.936	5.020	5.099	5.316	5.597	5.799	6.080	6.080
1976/77	4.253	4.325	4.393	4.580	4.822	4.996	5.238	5.238
1977/78	3.646	3.707	3.766	3.926	4.133	4.283	4.490	4.490
1978/79	3.368	3.425	3.479	3.627	3.819	3.956	4.148	4.148
1979/80	3.039	3.090	3.139	3.272	3.445	3.570	3.742	3.742
1980/81	2.631	2.675	2.718	2.833	2.983	3.091	3.240	3.240
1981/82	2.174	2.211	2.246	2.342	2.465	2.554	2.678	2.678
1982/83	1.829	1.860	1.890	1.970	2.074	2.149	2.253	2.253
1983/84	1.627	1.654	1.680	1.752	1.844	1.911	2.003	2.003
1984/85	1.477	1.502	1.525	1.590	1.674	1.735	1.819	1.819
1985/86	1.390	1.414	1.436	1.497	1.577	1.633	1.713	1.713
1986/87	1.330	1.352	1.373	1.432	1.507	1.562	1.637	1.637
1987/88	1.285	1.307	1.328	1.384	1.457	1.510	1.583	1.583
1988/89	1.261	1.282	1.303	1.358	1.430	1.481	1.553	1.553
1989/90	1.221	1.241	1.261	1.314	1.384	1.434	1.503	1.503
1990/91	1.171	1.191	1.210	1.261	1.328	1.376	1.442	1.442
1991/92	1.142	1.161	1.179	1.229	1.294	1.341	1.406	1.406
1992/93	1.101	1.120	1.138	1.186	1.249	1.294	1.356	1.356
1993/94	1.081	1.099	1.117	1.164	1.226	1.270	1.331	1.331
1994/95	1.063	1.081	1.098	1.144	1.205	1.248	1.309	1.309
1995/96	1.037	1.054	1.071	1.116	1.175	1.218	1.277	1.277
1996/97	1.016	1.033	1.050	1.094	1.152	1.194	1.251	1.251
1997/98	-	1.017	1.033	1.077	1.134	1.175	1.232	1.232
1998/99	-	-	1.016	1.059	1.115	1.156	1.212	1.212
1999/00	-	-	-	1.043	1.098	1.138	1.193	1.193
2000/01	-	-	-	-	1.053	1.091	1.144	1.144
2001	-	-	-	-	-	1.037	1.087	1.087
2002	-	-	-	-	-	-	1.049	1.049
2003	-	-	-	-	-	-	-	1.000
2004	-	-	-	-	-	-	-	1.000

Case Study: CGT liability on part rented property

You bought your home in January 1992 for €50,000. You rented it out from 31st December 1999 to 31st December 2003 while you worked abroad. You sold it in December 2004 for €200,000. Your CGT liability will be calculated as follows:

Period of Ownership:	
1st January 1992 - 31st December 1999	8 Years Principal Private Residence (PPR)
1st January 2000 - 31st December 2003	4 Years Rented
1st January 2004 - 31st December 2004	1 Year Deemed PPR - last 12 months of ownership
Total Period of ownership	13 Years
Non Principal Private Residence	4 Years

		Your position €
	Sale Price	€200,000
Less:	Selling Costs	(€2,000)
	Purchase Price	€50,000
	Indexation @ 1.406	€20,300
	Indexed Purchase Price	€70,300
	Capital Gain	€127,700
Less:	Capital Gains Exemption	(€1,270)
	Taxable Gain	€126,430
	Tax @ 20%	**€25,286**

However, you may claim CGT exemption for the eight years while the property was your main private residence, together with the last 12 months of ownership which is deemed to be your Principal Private Residence. So, your CGT liability will be €7,780 (4/13 x €25,286).

You could also claim total exemption from total CGT, provided you returned and lived in your former home for a period before you sold it.

Exit strategy

Property investing, remember, is all about making money. Some investors rarely sell. They ride the interest rate rollercoaster; they make due when the tenants pool seems a bit low; they grin and bear it when the market flattens. These investors are usually satisfied that over the long haul their property will achieve sufficient gain to justify their faith in the market. They also use their property or properties to fund other purchases and other investments.

Other property investors are more interested in shorter term gains. They are thrilled to buy a bargain, especially when interest rates are historically low, but they may not be as financially stable as they (or their bank manager) would like them to be. They may have used their family home to finance the buy-to-let. They could not easily weather a sharp interest rate hike or a property crash, however unlikely this may be here in the near future.

A word about property crashes (also see chapter 6). The UK bubble that burst so dramatically in the early 1990s was built very much on speculation, fuelled first by booming financial markets and relatively cheap money. The booming Irish market has been mainly based on low initial property prices and strong demand. The UK bubble was unsustainable because it did not have sufficient demand.

Ireland's economy going forward, at least to the end of this decade, will be fuelled by large numbers of transient workers who intend to remain for a few years and will need rental accommodation. There is also expected to be a relatively steady stream of first time buyers though the high building rate (c. 77,000 new house in 2004) will drop over the same period.

As part of your exit strategy you need to consider the following:

- Are you buying the investment property as a long term holding? If you are buying as a nest egg or as something to hand to children, then stay the course of the 20 years it takes for the mortgage to be cleared.

- If you have built up a portfolio of properties, selling one or two out of a stock of seven could help clear the mortgages on all or most of the others, producing a clear profit from the remaining rent.

- You must continually monitor the market for any signs of slowdowns or busts usually precipitated by rising interest rates or unemployment. This is so that you can act promptly, either by selling, or if the collapse does happen suddenly, by reducing your rent to ensure your property is fully let as the rental market becomes more competitive.

It is said you can never lose with bricks and mortar, and this is generally true. But it is never truer than when you have spread your portfolio – and risk - over a number of markets, both domestic and foreign.

With two or more properties, one can always be sacrificed if there is downturn, in order to maintain the other until that mortgage is cleared. With two properties and retirement looming, the rental income or even the sale of one of the properties can produce the sole pension income.

Insuring your investment property

Insurance in Ireland is very expensive compared to other European countries. However, you should resist the temptation to underinsure your investment property as this will cost you dearly if there is a fire or major damage to the house or apartment.

In apartment complexes the management company fees will generally cover the buildings. You will have to insure the fittings but not your tenant's contents. With a house, you will have to insure both. This expense can be offset against tax so shop around. If you have a number of properties, negotiate with your insurer to see if they will offer you a group deal.

Direct investing in property is all very well, but it comes at a price. Purchase costs, which include everything from survey and legal fees to Stamp Duty and/or sales taxes can easily add another 10% to the cost of the investment. The property then needs to be fitted and furnished, it needs to be insured and there may on ongoing management and maintenance fees. It can take a great deal of time – and anxious moments - to physically buy the property if it goes to auction, for example.

Property Funds

An alternative form of property investing is through professionally managed investment funds, which are increasingly popular in this country as private pension assets for the self-employed and company directors. These deals are very tax efficient with tax relief available on both the pension contributions and mortgage payments.

Property already makes up a part of most managed pension funds in Ireland, though it only represents about 5% of the asset under management in such a portfolio. Though some analysts would argue that this weighting is too low, many individual investors have pushed up their exposure to property by buying a second home or investment property. Since the average person in Ireland has not heavily invested in formal pension funds, anyone with two or more properties is proportionately heavily exposed to the vagaries of this single investment market.

Average performance

The average Irish property fund, managed by Irish fund managers has returned annual gross returns of +16% over the past 10 years. Over five and three years, the returns are +10.8% and over the past year +11.8%. While these returns are certainly much lower in recent years, the first quarter of this 2005 have still returned +2.8% growth; if this performance was repeated for each of the remaining three quarters the annual gross return would be down just +0.6% on 2004.

Compared to the five year returns for other asset classes like equities (-7.5%) and cash funds (+8.1%), Irish property funds have performed very well indeed.

Property	Qtr 1 %	1 Yr %	3 Yrs (p.a.) %	5 Yrs (p.a.) %	10 Yrs (p.a.) %
AIBIM	**4.6**	**15.6**	**10.5**	11.2	**17.6**
BIAM	**2.8**	**10.8**	**8.1**	10.0	**15.5**
Canada Life / Setanta	**1.4**	**8.1**	**13.1**	10.2	**13.8**
Friends First /F&C	**1.8**	**11.2**	**15.3**	**13.6**	**17.9**
Hibernian Life *	**0.9**	**9.3**	**8.6**	**7.7**	**13.7**
Hibernian Life **	**4.7**				
Irish Life	**4.1**	**13.3**	**9.7**	**11.8**	**17.4**
IPUT	**4.7**	**13.5**	**11.0**	**10.9**	**16.1**
New Ireland	**0.2**	**10.4**	**9.0**	**10.3**	**15.5**
Average	**2.8**	**11.8**	**10.8**	**10.8**	**16.0**
Standard Life Investments	**0.7**	**10.9**	**8.6**	**10.2**	**15.6**

*** this fund is closed to new business**

**** New Business with Hibernian is allocated into this fund**

Friends First

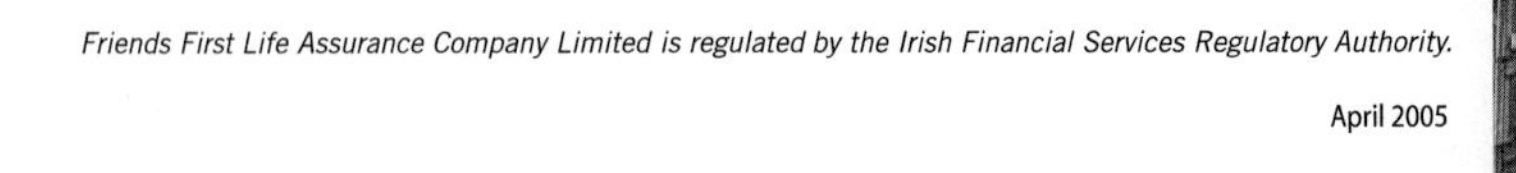

There are many specialised geographical property funds now available too, rather than the conventional ones in which individual commercial, retail or industrial properties in the Ireland or the UK (or a mixture of both) are managed by the investment firm's specialist managers. There include lower cost property fund indices, including the well known European Property Real Estate Association Index (EPREA) which is comprised of 70 of Europe's biggest publicly quoted property companies across 14 European countries.

Funds like these are available from the investment divisions of Irish life assurance companies and the bank assurers, as well as directly from fund management companies. Indexed property funds that trade on world stock markets in the form of ETFs, or exchange traded funds, can be bought directly from a stockbroker, in the same way you can buy a single share.

Cost of property funds

The cost of these funds varies. Some persist with upfront charges like 'bid offer spreads', usually amounting to 5% of your capital. Others charge less or dispense altogether with upfront charges depending on the size of your investment, though they often include an exit penalty on a scale of between 1% and 5% of the value of your fund if you encash at any time in the first five years. The annual management fee for a managed property fund is usually between 0.75% and 2% per annum, a charge that can have a very dramatic effect on your fund in a falling market. Indexed property funds, which are passively managed, are even better value, with lower entry and exit charges (if any) and lower annual management fees.

Many property funds are now 'geared' which allows the fund manager to borrow a multiple of the fund value, represented by your money and all the other investors', to purchase a higher value portfolio of properties. Gearing adds a certainly amount of extra risk to your investment (and potentially greater rewards) since the fund will be more exposed to falling prices. You need to have faith in the skill and expertise of your fund manager before you buy into such a geared fund.

The best performing Irish managed property fund for the last three, five and ten years is the Friends First fund with annualised returns of 17.9%. Anyone who had invested €50,000 in this fund over the last five years would have earned a gross return to date of €114,000. Over a ten year period the gross return would be nearly €260,000.

Like any other kind of investment fund, a property fund is going to be cyclical. Property returns are sensitive to interest rate increases, employment trends, supply and demand and overheated markets.

Property speculating on a global scale has certainly inflated the price of residential and holiday homes in many countries. Prices don't always keep going upward, (see chapter 6) so treat this kind of property investment with the same consideration as you would a direct purchase:

- Make sure to research the product and underlying properties in the fund carefully with your financial advisor.
- Be clear about your financial expectations, targets and risk profile.
- Determine how long you want to tie up your money in this fund.
- Take a hard look at all fees and charges associated with this product and compare these with other funds.
- Accept that property funds can and will fall as well as rise in value just like any other asset over the course of a 10 year or longer investment period.
- Check for exit penalties if you encash your fund early (say, within the first five years).

Historically – and by this we mean over very long periods - property as an asset class has not performed as well as stocks and shares, but it is considered a secure port of call for investor's money. Concentrating as they do on mainly commercial properties (though larger residential developments have a place in property funds), professionally managed property funds are taking an educated bet on the wider economic parameters in a city or country and on having long term leases in place with by credible, corporate tenants.

One thing is certain: professional fund managers are not prone to the flights of whimsy that overcome some amateur property investors, who make wild decisions to hand over substantial down payments during weekend property shows to dodgy, unregulated salesmen selling seaside villas in Bulgaria.

Small self administered pension plans (SSAP's)

As a result of the Finance Act 2004 and changes in the Revenue Commissioners' practice on pension arrangements, you can now borrow to acquire assets for investment purposes, giving rise to what is termed Geared Property Pensions.

The Geared Property Pension is particularly attractive for proprietary directors who wish to use their company pension to purchase a commercial property or 'buy to let' residential property as it allows the company to borrow in order to finance the purchase. Acquiring property directly through your pension fund has the attraction over the personal investment in property in that surplus rents are not taxed and properties can be sold free of Capital Gains Tax. It also gives you greater control over your investment and running costs can be clearly established.

In order to take advantage of these borrowing changes, you must set up a Self-Administered Pensions Scheme with an advisor who is a recognised pension trustee, though this does attract additional administration and accounting charges, compared to conventional pension fund investments.

The following is a summary of the attractions of setting up a self administered pension plan/trust:

- It is possible to invest in a range of properties.
- It is suitable for proprietary directors.

- All transfers to the self administered retirement trust is tax deductible by the company.
- Directors are not liable to tax on the transfers.
- Directors have control over their own pension.
- It is a tax efficient way to pass wealth to the next generation.
- Borrowing is permitted under the Finance Act 2004.

Geared pension funds are not suitable for everyone and you should always consult with your advisor before making any changes to your existing pension arrangements.

Chapter 5

5

Property Tax Incentives

Property tax incentives

Property tax incentives fall into two main areas: capital allowances relating to industrial buildings and tax incentives relating to designated areas. Most of the tax incentives available on property are due to cease on the 31s July 2006. When buying a property on which tax incentives apply you should ensure that it makes commercial sense even without the tax breaks. Also make sure when buying a section 23 property that you have adequate rental income to absorb the relief available on the section 23 property. There's not much point in paying for a tax designated investment if you then find you can't use the allowances.

Qualifying industrial buildings

Section 268 of the Taxes Consolidation Act 1997 sets out the type of industrial buildings or structures which qualify for relief. These are, a building or structure in use:

- For the purposes of a trade carried on in a mill, factory or other similar premises, or a laboratory the sole or main function of which is the analysis of minerals in connection with exploration for or extraction of such minerals.
- For the purposes of a dock undertaking.
- For the purpose of growing fruit, vegetables in the trade of market gardening.
- For the purpose of the trade of hotel-keeping.

- For the purpose of intensive production of cattle, sheep, pigs, poultry, or eggs in the course of a trade, other than farming.
- For the purpose of a trade which consists of the operation or management of an airport and which is an airport runway or an airport apron used solely or mainly by aircraft carrying passengers or cargo for hire or reward.
- For the purpose of a trade which consists of the operation or management of a qualifying nursing home.
- For the purpose of a trade which consists of the operation or management of a qualifying convalescent home (such convalescent home must hold a certificate from the relevant Health Board) for the provision of medical and nursing care or persons recovering from a treatment in a hospital which provides treatment for acutely ill patients.

The type of allowance available include:

1. Initial allowance: An initial allowance is available in the case where a person incurred capital expenditure on the construction of an industrial building or structure which is occupied for the purpose of a trade. The initial allowance is available to both owner-occupiers and lessors. These allowances were severely restricted over the years and were eliminated for capital expenditure incurred after 31st March 1992 except in certain cases. e.g. buildings in designated areas.

2. Annual allowance: An annual allowance is generally available to persons holding an interest in an industrial building or structure. The rate varies between 4% and 15% depending on the type of trade for which the industrial building or structure is being used. The annual allowance is available to both owner-occupiers and lessors of buildings. Nursing homes, convalescent homes and crèche facilities will normally qualify for a 15% annual allowance on qualifying expenditure for the first six years and 10% in year seven.

3. Capital Allowances on hotels and holiday camps are allowed at 4% per annum for 25 years. Capital allowances on holiday cottages will no longer be available from 4th December 2002 unless full planning permission was received by 31st May 2003. In this case the termination date is 31st July 2006.

Most other industrial buildings will normally qualify at an annual rate of 4% p.a. over a 25 year period.

Holiday cottages

As a result of Finance Act 2003, a registered holiday cottage will no longer be regarded as a building in use for the trade of hotel keeping. On this basis, registered holiday cottages will no longer qualify for capital allowances.

Also, the wear and tear rate for capital expenditure incurred on a hotel building is reduced to 4% per annum.

These changes apply for capital expenditure incurred on or after 31st July 2006 on the construction and refurbishment of a building where an application for planning application is made on or before 10th March 2002 in accordance with the Local Government (Planning and Development) Regulations 1994, or on or before 31st December 2004 in accordance with Planning and Development Regulations 2001 to 2002.

Where a planning permission application is not made before the deadlines, the changes will be effective from 4th December 2002.

Some registered Holiday cottages are still available, which attract Capital Allowances at a rate of 10% per annum.

Designated Areas

In 1986, areas were defined as 'designated' for property investing tax relief purposes in each of the five cities of Cork, Dublin, Galway, Limerick and Waterford. Areas are designated by order of the Minister for the Environment and Local Government, with the consent of the Minister for Finance under the Urban Renewal Act, 1986. These urban renewal schemes were subsequently extended to include areas in many of Ireland's major towns.

1994 Urban Renewal Scheme

The 1994 scheme was more focused than its predecessor, concentrating on those areas where dereliction was most severe and providing for greater remedial works and measures to conserve existing urban infrastructure. More emphasis was placed on residential development in inner urban areas to provide a better mix of social and private housing and a greater use of vacant upper floors.

1999 Urban Renewal Scheme

Following an in-depth consultancy study on the operation of urban renewal schemes, the Government introduced a major new urban renewal scheme in 1999. The scheme, which benefited five cities and 38 towns represented a more targeted approach to urban renewal incentives, concentrating not just on areas of physical development but also on issues of local socio-economic benefits.

The termination date was extended to 31st July 2006 in respect of the 1999 Urban Renewal Scheme, provided 15% of the total project cost had been incurred by 30th June 2003. Application for certification must have been submitted to the local authority by 31st July 2003 and certification must have been issued by 30th September 2003.

Town Renewal Scheme

Town Renewal Schemes are based on a similar approach to that which applies in relation to the 1999 Urban Renewal Scheme. Designations are based on Town Renewal Plans (TRPs) which in turn were based on the principles of promoting the physical renewal and revitalisation of towns, enhancing their amenities and promoting sustainable development patterns. The termination date for the Town Renewal Scheme has been extended to 31st July 2006 provided full planning application has been received by the relevant planning authority by 31st December 2004.

Rural Renewal Relief

This relief was introduced in the 1998 Finance Act. It designated parts of Cavan, Roscommon and Sligo and the administrative county of Leitrim and Longford.

The deadline for the Rural and Urban Renewal Schemes for tax relief for expenditure on commercial, industrial and residential projects has been extended to 31st December 2004. The termination date for Rural Renewal Relief was extended to 31st July 2006 provided full planning application has been received by the relevant planning authority by 31st December 2004.

Tax Summary

Below, we summarise the tax incentives available to owner occupiers and investors for urban, town and rural renewal schemes.

Residential - owner occupier	• **Construction:** **5% deduction against total income for 10 years.** • **Refurbishment:** **10% deduction against total income for 10 years**
	• **Section 23- type relief in respect of expenditure on the construction, conversion or refurbishment expenditure.**
Non residential - owner occupier	• **Free depreciation - 50%** • **Initial allowances - 50%** • **Annual allowance for 12 years - 4%**
Non residential - investor	• **Initial allowance - 50% Year 1** • **Annual allowance for 121/2 years - 4%**

Section 23 Residential investment

Section 23 type relief is available on the construction, conversion and refurbishment of certain residential premises in designated areas.

The minimum floor area for a house is 35 square metres and the maximum area is 125 square metres. The minimum floor area for a flat or maisonette is 30 square metres and the maximum area is 90 square metres. The property must be used solely as a dwelling and cannot be owner-occupied within 10 years of the first letting. If, however, within the 10 year period, the property ceases to be a qualifying premises e.g. is sold or owner-occupied, all the allowances already given will be clawed back. If a qualifying property is sold within the 10 year period and is then rented, the purchaser will be entitled to the same allowance as the original owner. There is no restriction on the amount of rent which may be charged, but the property must be let under a qualifying lease. i.e. the lease must be a genuine rental agreement with regular payments by way of rent and the tenant cannot be granted an option to buy the property at less than the market value.

Qualifying expenditure

If you buy a qualifying property in a designated area, the site cost together with a portion of the builder's profit is not allowed as qualifying expenditure.

Qualifying expenditure is arrived at by applying the formula:

$$\text{Purchase Price} \quad \times \quad \frac{\text{Builder's Development Cost}}{\text{Site Cost + Builder's Development Cost}}$$

	€
Cost of Site	€45,000
Development Costs	€230,000
Builder's Profit	€25,000
Purchase Price	€300,000

Qualifying expenditure is as follows:

$$€300,000 \times \frac{€230,000}{€45,000 + €230,000} = €250,909$$

This €250,909 is available to offset against all taxable rental income.

	Without Section 23 €	With Section 23 €
Taxable Rental Income	€30,000	€30,000
"Section 27" relief	-	€250,909
Tax Payable @ 42%	€12,600	Nil
Rental Loss to be carried forward to the following year	Nil	€220,909

Buying a second hand "Section 23" property

If you buy a property where the qualifying expenditure has already been claimed, all relief already granted to the original owner will be clawed back and passed on to you, provided you rent a property and the property is less than 10 years old.

The non-residential investor

Gerard is a small business person and he has considerable faith in retail property in his town which is finally seeing inward investment and is also well supported by local industry. He bought a site in a designated area for €1,000,000. The qualifying building expenditure at December 2004 was €600,000. His tax rate is 42%. Gerard's tax savings are as follows:

	€
Development Cost	€600,000
Capital Allowances 50% in Year 1	€300,000
Tax Saving @ 42%	€126,000

He will also get a €24,000 Annual Allowance for years 2 to 13 and an annual allowance of €12,000 in year 14. These annual allowances will be granted at his marginal rate of tax

Double rent allowance for traders

A trader is entitled to a tax allowance of double the rent payable for an industrial or commercial building in a designated area if the lease has been negotiated during the qualifying period. The allowance is available for a period of 10 years. The relief does not apply unless the building is let on bona fide commercial terms to an unconnected person.

However, the maximum amount of capital allowances which you can offset against your total income has been capped at €31,750 in any one year for investors. This cap does not affect owner occupiers or active partners.

Current Incentives Schemes

Scheme	Qualifying Period	Floor Area
Integrated area	1st August 1998 to 31st July 2006 urban renewal. If 15% certificate not issued, end date is 31st December 2004. (See note 1)	Not less than 38 square metres and note more than 125 square metres.
Town renewal	1st April 2000 to 31st July 2006. If full and valid planning application not submitted on or before 31st December 2004, end date is 31st December 2004	Not less than 28 square metres and not more than 125 square metres or in the case of a conversion or refurbishment expenditure incurred on or after 6th April 2001
Rural renewal	6th April 1999 to 31st July 2006. If full and valid planning application not submitted on or before 31st December 2004, end date is 31st December 2004	Not less than 38 square metres and not more than 210 square metres
Living over the shop	6th April 2001 to 31st July 2006. If full and valid planning application not submitted on or before 31st December 2004, end date is 31st December 2004.	Not less than 38 square metres and not more than 125 square metres.
Park and ride	1st July 1999 to 31st July 2006 If full and valid planning application not submitted on or before 31st December 2004, end date is 31st December 2004	Not less than 38 square metres and not more than 125 square metres.
Note: The termination date was originally extended from 31 December 2002 to 31st December 2004 where 15% of the total project cost was incurred by 31st December 2002, and a local authority certificate to this effect was issued by 30th April 2003. These dates were later changed; the current position is that 15% of the total project cost must be incurred by 30th June 2003, and the local authority certificate to this effect must be issued by 30th September 2003.		

Integrated area Urban Renewal Scheme

City/County Area/Town

Cork	**Blackpool/Shandon City Docks Area**
Dublin	**Ballymum, HARP, Inchicore /Kilmainham, Liberties/Coombe, North East Inner City, Millennium/O'Connell St**
Galway	**3 surburban local authority estates**
Limerick	**1 large central area**
Waterford	**Periphery of commercial centre**
Carlow	**Carlow**
Clare	**Shannon**
Cork	**Bandon, Cobh, Mallow (N),Passage West(S)/Glenbrook**
Donegal	**Buncrana**
Dublin	**Dun Laoghaire, Balbriggan, North West Blanchardstown, North Clondalkin, Tallaght**
Galway	**Tuam**
Kerry	**Tralee**
Kildare	**Athy, Kildare**
Kilkenny	**Kilkenny**
Laois	**Portlaoise**
Limerick	**Newcastlewest**
Longford	**Longford**
Mayo	**Ballina**

Meath	**Navan**
Monaghan	**Monaghan**
Offaly	**Birr, Tullamore, Clara**
Sligo	**Sligo**
Tipperary	**Roscrea, Thurles, Carrick-on-Suir, Tipperary**
Waterford	**Dungarvan**
Westmeath	**Athlone, Mullingar**
Wexford	**New Ross**
Wicklow	**Arklow, Wicklow.**
Louth	**Drogheda, Dundalk**

Rural Renewal Scheme - Qualifying County Areas

Cavan	The District Electoral Divisions of Arvagh, Springfield, Killashandra, Milltown, Carrafin, Grilly, Kilconny, Belturbet Urban, Ardue, Carn, Bilberry, Diamond, Doogary, Lissanover, Ballymagauran, Ballyconnell, Bawnboy, Templeport, Benbrack, Pedara Vohers, Tircahan, Swanlinbar, Kinawley, Derrynananta, Dunmakeever, Dowra, Derrylahan, Tuam, Killinagh, Eskey,Teebane, Scrabby, Loughdawan, Bruce Hall, Drumcarban, Corr, Crossdoney, and Killykeen.
Leitrim	The administrative county of Leitrim.
Longford	The administrative county of Longford.
Roscommon	The District Electoral Divisions of Ballintober, Castleteheen, Carrowduff, Kilbride North, Lissonuffy, Killavackan, Termonbarry, Roosky, Kilglass North, Kilglass South, Bumlin, Cloonfinlough, Killukin (in Roscommon Rural District), Strokestown, Annaghmore, Tulsk, Coolougher, Ballinlough, Kiltullagh,Cloonfower, Artagh South, Artagh North, Ballaghaderreen,Edmondstown, Loughglinn, Buckill, Fairymount, Castlereagh,Frenchpark, Bellangare, Castleplunket, Baslick, Breedoge,Altagowlan, Lough Allen, Ballyfarnan, Keadue, Aghafin,Ballyformoyle, Crossna, Kilbryan, Boyle Rural, Boyle Urban, Tivannagh, Rushfield, Tumna North, Tumna South, Killukin (in Boyle No. 1 Rural District), Oakport, Rockingham, Danesfort, Cloonteem, Kilmore, Elia, Ballygarden, Aughrim East, Aughrim, West, Creeve (in Boyle No. 1 Rural District), Creeve (in Roscommon Rural District), Elphin, Rossmore, Cloonyquinn, Ogulla, Mantua, Lisgarve, Kilmacumsy, Kilcolagh, Estersnow, Croghan, Killummod, Cregga, Cloonygormican, Kilbride South,Kilgefin, Cloontuskert, Drumdaff, and Kilteevan.
Sligo	The District Electoral Divisions of Ballintogher East, Ballynakill, Lisconny, Drumfin, Ballymote, Cloonoghill, Leitrim, Tobercurry, Kilturra, Cuilmore, Kilfree, Coolavin, Killaraght, Templevanny, Aghanagh, Kilmactranny, Ballynashee, Shancough, Drumcolumb, Riverstown, Lakeview, Bricklieve, Drumrat, Toomour, Kilshalvy, Killadoon, Streamstown, Cartron, Coolaney, Owenmore, Temple, Annagh, Carrickbannagher, Collooney, and Ballintogher West.

Town Renewal Scheme – Designated County Towns

Carlow	Hacketstown, Muinbheag, Tullow, Tinnahinch/Graiguenamanagh
Cavan	Cavan, Cootehill, Baileborough, Ballyjamesduff
Clare	Scarriff, Sixmilebridge, Kilrush, Miltown Malbay, Ennistymon
Cork	Cloyne, Skibbereen, Charleville (Rathluirc), Doneraile, Kanturk, Bantry, Fermoy
Donegal	Moville, Ardara, Ramelton, Ballyshannon, Ballybofey, Stranorlar
Galway	Portumna, Headford, Loughrea, Clifden, Ballygar
Kerry	Listowel, Castleisland, Killorglin, Caherciveen
Kildare	Kilcullen, Castledermot, Rathangan, Kilcock, Monasterevan
Kilkenny	Callan, Castlecomer, Thomastown, Urlingford, Pilltown
Laois	Mountrath, Rathdowney, Portarlington, Mountmellick
Limerick	Abbeyfeale, Castleconnell, Croom, Kilmallock, Rathkeale
Louth	Carlingford, Ardee, Dunleer, Castlebellingham
Mayo	Ballinrobe, Belmullet, Claremorris, Foxford, Newport
Meath	Oldcastle, Duleek, Kells, Trim
Monaghan	Clones, Castleblayney, Ballybay
Offaly	Clara, Ferbane, Edenderry, Banagher
Roscommon	Roscommon
Sligo	Rosses Point, Bellaghy-Charlestown
Tipperary N.R	Nenagh, Templemore, Borrisokane, Littleton
Tipperary S.R.	Cashel, Killenaule, Cahir, Fethard
Waterford	Cappoquin, Portlaw, Kilmacthomas, Tallow
Westmeath	Kilbeggan, Castlepollard, Moate
Waterford	Ferns, Bunclody, Taghmon, Gorey
Wicklow	Dunlavin, Rathdrum, Carnew, Baltinglass, Tinahely

6

Buying, selling and letting

There is considerable art - and skill - involved in the process of buying, selling and letting property, which is why estate agents and property managers are so successful. Many more properties are sold here with the professional assistance of estate agents than are sold privately by owners, but understanding the buying and selling process is important if you want to maximise the price you sell your own property for and hopefully, minimise the price you pay for someone else's.

Location, appearance and demand play a major part in the prices that certain properties command, and explain the huge rise in house prices in Ireland in the past decade. But knowing how to present your property in its best light should result in the two things that every seller wants – a quick sale and the best price.

This chapter looks at all aspects of the buying, selling and letting process, from choosing an estate agent or devising your own selling campaign, auctions, and what happens when the time comes to make or accept a bid.

The buyer

Buying property, whether as a home, or as an investment is both an exciting and nerve-wracking experience. The amount of money involved is enormous and mistakes will be very costly to put right, whether caused by choosing the wrong mortgage or overspending on renovations and repairs to a derelict buy-to-let project.

Consider the following checklist when you set out to buy any property:

- Does the property fulfil your basic needs such as its location to work, schools, shops, amenities and transport?
- Is the size of the property adequate for your needs or desires, or will it need to be extended to accommodate your existing or future family? How much will an extension cost? Is this affordable?
- Does the property require immediate renovation/ repair or redecoration and how much will this cost?
- What is the exact size of the property and does the price per square metre match the advertised price/size?
- Before you make a bid, a surveyor should be hired to produce a detailed report of the property. The survey should include not just an examination of the roof and foundations, but the wiring, plumbing, heating, whether there is evidence of insect infestation, dry and wet rot, subsidence, radon gas and whether the drains work efficiently.
- Is there an energy efficiency certificate available?
- Is a tax clearance certificate available? If the property is worth more than €500,000 and a Capital Gains clearance certificate CG50A is not provided by the seller, you are obliged to send 15% of the purchase price to the Revenue Commissioners.
- How much are annual service charges and other applicable property taxes?
- How much are annual utility costs, maintenance charges and management fees? This is particularly applicable for rental or holiday properties.
- Are there development plans for the area? Is a new road, apartments or a recycling centre being planned for the area? Traffic congestion and pollution are two of the most common repercussions of new development and you should check with the local authority for any plans that might impact on your new house.

- If you are buying a new property you may be required to pay a booking deposit to the builder or developer. This deposit is always refundable up to the contract stage.

- Find a good solicitor or inquire whether your mortgage advisor offers legal conveyancing as part of their service.

- How much will insurance for the property cost? This includes mortgage protection life insurance and buildings/contents insurance.

The seller

Consider the following checklist when setting out to sell a property:

- Seek out at least three professional valuations (without an instruction to sell) before setting your asking price and do your own research of house prices in your neighbourhood.

- Establish exactly what items are for sale with the house, such as made-to-measure curtains and carpets, light fittings, garden equipment and furniture, appliances (dishwasher/washing-machine, etc) or furniture.

- Be aware of any structural or other faults and set your price accordingly as these will more than likely be revealed by the buyer's survey.

- Prepare a proper description of the house to give to an estate agent who will sell the house or an even more detailed one if you intend to sell the house yourself, without the services of an agent. This description should include not just what kind of house it is (semi-detached, terrace, etc) and how many rooms it has, but its age, square footage, special architectural or other features (such as a fine garden), whether it is freehold or leasehold, and a description of neighbourhood amenities and public transport.

- Prepare a list of all the repair and decorative jobs to be done. Ask a friend whose judgement and taste you trust to give their objective opinion about the state of the paintwork and garden. Hiring a professional painter to redecorate key rooms and a cleaning company could be money well spent to achieve the sparkling finish that will enhance the selling price.

- If your property is worth more than €500,000 you are required to provide the buyer with a CG50A tax clearance certificate otherwise they must send 15% of the purchase price to the Revenue Commissioners.

Use an Agent or DIY?

Estate agents fees amount to approximately 2% of the selling price plus 21% VAT, plus optional extra costs for advertising or 'show' days.

A typical house with a selling price of €350,000 will therefore cost the owner a minimum of €7,000 plus VAT of €1,470 for a total of €8,470. This charge is going to escalate if you are also buying a new house and are faced with a stiff Stamp Duty bill as well.

The majority of sellers opt for a sales agent because the hassle of selling is taken out of their hands. The agent will be familiar with the prices that have been achieved in your neighbourhood; they will erect the signs on your lawn, prepare the brochure, place the advertisements and notices in the newspapers and internet sites (usually at an additional cost) and arrange to show your house, both to individuals or during a public viewing. They want to sell your house as quickly as you do as this increases their turnover and profit.

They can also provide a good deal of advice about how to enhance the property for the maximum price and can point you in the direction of property 'dressers' or furniture rental agencies who can store your shabby sofas and beds and replace them during the selling period with stylish items that show off your house in its best light.

The estate agent or auctioneer is acting on your behalf, as well as their own, and is there to help you set the appropriate guide price, which, in the case of a sale by auction, should be within 10% of your reserve price under guidelines set by the Irish Auctioneers and Valuers Institute (IAVI).

If your property is sold by 'Private Treaty' your agent can help you negotiate with bidders; if there is more than one interested party they may suggest that bids be submitted in writing 'by tender' though you are not obliged to accept any offer made this way.

Once you and the buyer agree a price, your solicitor will draw up a contract of sale which is sent to the buyer's solicitor who will determine whether it is satisfactory or not. The buyer then signs the contract subject to all miscellaneous conditions being agreed. A minor issue, for example, might be whether the buyer wishes to buy items such as curtains or appliances, garden furniture, etc. This pre-contract period can take up to a month as the buyer's solicitor proceeds with the detailed title search and examination. A deed to transfer the title from the seller to buyer is then drawn up by the buyer's solicitor and if accepted by your solicitor it is then sent back to the buyer's solicitor for 'engrossment', which prepares the final deed for signature.

Most solicitors suggest that buyers do a final check of the property before they sign any final contract, so you can expect at least one more visit from the buyer. The property and any items being sold with it should be in the same condition – that is, undamaged and intact – as they were when the purchase offer was made.

Once the sale is closed, the deed is signed and the bank draft (never a personal cheque) is handed over; your house is now sold. Before then however, you will need to agree a completion date. Be prepared for some haggling since there may be other transactions at stake and a property chain can be a perilous thing if it is too long. It is important that all parties are clear as to exactly when your house – soon to be their house - will be vacant. Ideally, two sets of removal vans should not be parked outside the one property on the same day!

Sell by Auction

Selling by auction is a popular alternative to the private treaty or tender system, especially in a strong selling market and in particular for higher value, unique or period properties.

The cost of selling by auction usually amounts to 1.5% - 2% of the property value plus VAT at 21% plus additional services such as advertising and promotions. As with private treaty transactions, and legal charges, this figure is negotiable and you should shop around to find an auctioneer willing to charge a lower fee.

If you opt to sell by auction, you should establish a guide price, within 10% of the reserve that will be set on the auction day, though guide and even reserve prices can, and are frequently exceeded. Auctioneers provide potential bidders with a document known as the 'conditions of sale' and it is available to the buyer and their solicitor to examine prior to the auction. Aside from the buyer's solicitor checking to ensure that the deed is in order, a serious bidder should have also arranged for a survey of your property to be undertaken before attending the auction.

The auction must be informed once the reserve price is met but if it is not, the property can be withdrawn and private negotiations can proceed. At the end of a successful auction, the person who has successfully bid for your property must sign a contract that also sets the closing date of the sale and pay a 10% deposit.

Buying at auction

If you decide to bid for an auctioned property, you need to do all the same research and preparation as you would for a private treaty sale. This means:

- Ensuring that the location is suitable for your needs and budget.
- Checking out the amenities, schools, shops and transport in the area.
- Arranging for a thorough survey of the property.

Owners who go the auction route do say because of the higher prices achieved, but the fact that the final sale price often exceeds the guide price by a quarter or more, is very contentious with many auction goers who have spent time and money arranging for surveys for properties which end up being far more expensive than they were led to believe. Don't get caught attending auctions in which you have not factored in this anomaly.

Many bidders ask their solicitor to accompany them to the auction, sometimes both to do the bidding (and to keep within budget), to assist in closing the sale if the bid is successful or to negotiate privately afterwards if the property has been withdrawn because it did not meet its reserve price.

The most important thing about attending an auction is to be clear in your own mind about how much you are willing to pay for this property. Having a price ceiling, that you stick to, means you will not get caught in the auction fever so beloved by sellers and auctioneers. Just keep reminding yourself of this version of an old adage: 'Buy in haste, repent at your leisure'.

For Sale by Owner?

The number of 'For Sale' signs in your neighbourhood and the speed with which houses sell is a pretty good indicator of how quickly your own property will sell.

If you are convinced that yours is a desirable house/neighbourhood and you have the time and determination to spare, you could consider selling your house without the use of professional agent or auctioneer. This is known in America, where it is far more popular because of the much higher estate agent fee - often as high as 6% - as 'FSBO' or For Sale by Owner.

Selling your house requires a proper marketing campaign. We suggest the following:

- Have a number of professional valuations, with no commitment to sell, done of your house by local estate agents. Use the average figure as your guide price.

- Do your own research of your neighbourhood by visiting other, similar, houses for sale. Not only will you get a feel for the prices being achieved in the area, but of the physical and decorative condition that you must match or exceed to secure a better price.

- Draw up an inventory of everything you are willing to sell in addition to the house: fitted curtains and carpets, appliances, garden equipment and furniture, furniture and special lighting fixtures (like crystal chandeliers) and then set a price.

- Work out a budget. By selling your house yourself you are aiming to save the estate agent's fee, but you must be prepared to spend some money to mount a successful selling campaign. Include the cost of advertisements in local and national newspapers, internet sites, signage, flyers and brochures, legal fees, redecoration.

- Write a clear and detailed description of the house, garden and environs for your information and for that of serious bidders who may look for more details. This includes the measurements of all the rooms, the size of the windows, the number of electric sockets and radiators; the location of cable television and telephone sockets. You can also include a description of the neighbourhood, its services and amenities, such as the nearest shops, churches, schools, the bus routes and frequency, the nearest doctor's surgery and Garda station, whether there is a neighbourhood watch or resident's association.

- The feature sheet that you give out to visitors should include basic information, such as location, number of rooms, size, whether it has gas or electric central heating, a security system and finished attic but not necessarily the exact dimensions of every room. You want people to ask questions, and to be able to offer them more information. The information sheet you hand out should remind them of the special features of your house such as the bay windows in the living room or the French doors to the garden or being on a Luas line. Mention the designer kitchen and the beautiful Adam-style fireplace or the prominent flower or shrub collections in the garden. Consider including colour photographs of the rooms and garden.

- Write a newspaper and/or internet advertisement and book the ads.
- Prepare a flyer that describes your property. This can be distributed door to door in your immediate neighbourhood. Put notices up in local shops and supermarkets.
- Put up a 'For Sale' sign on your own property. If you live on a cul-de-sac, or down a country road, find out if you can put up an sign on the busier, main road that directs buyers to your house.
- Do a room-by-room inventory of the house for repair and decoration purposes.
- De-clutter. Take at least one piece of furniture out of every room and store it with family, friends or in a rented lock-up. Do not leave any valuables or knic-knacs lying around when showing the property, and especially not during open viewings.
- Consider hiring a team of professional cleaners. Fitted carpets should be steam cleaned professionally.
- Consider – within budget - hiring a firm of house 'dressers' or a furniture rental service to help present your house in its best light during the selling period.
- Decide whether to show the house by appointment, through open viewings or a combination of the two. A 'virtual tour' website can be a very useful selling tool. Make sure you identify every visitor by providing a visitor's book to sign. Arrange for a helper to be present (this is for security purposes too) but children and pets should be kept occupied elsewhere.
- You will still need the services of a solicitor to complete the sale. Give the solicitor a copy of your house deeds, mortgage contract, etc. Make sure to ask about their fee before you hire them.

When a bid has been received, you will have to negotiate with the buyer(s). If there is more than one buyer offering the asking price you can hold a tender asking for their 'best and final offer' in writing. You are not obliged to reveal the tender offers and you are still under no obligation to accept any of the offers.

Once you have accepted a bid, your solicitor and their solicitor will hopefully spring to action: a deposit will be taken. The buyer's solicitor will do a thorough search of the title and deeds; negotiations will take place about any other items the buyer may wish to purchase from your inventory, and if all goes well with your respective lenders you should be ready to exchange and sign contracts within four to six weeks.

Once the sale is complete

It is now time to take possession of your new home. Moving house is a stress-filled event so consider the following checklist to reduce the hassle:

- Check out removal companies or van rental firms early in the buying/selling process and include the estimated cost in your moving budget. Find out how much notice the removals firm will need to schedule your move.

- If you are doing your own packing make sure to gather together enough packing cases, cardboard boxes, old newspapers and other packing materials in advance of your move.

- Contact the utility companies – telephone, electricity and gas to cancel your existing service and to transfer your name to the new property account. If you are moving into a house that has been empty, with no electricity connection for between six months and two years you will need to have it checked out by an electrical contractor and secure a new ETCI certificate. A new connection will need to be applied for if the house has been without electricity for more than two years.

- If your house needs to be connected to gas mains that are more than 15 metres away it will cost you at least €250 plus VAT at 13.5% plus an additional €73.78 per extra metre. A connection fee of c.€127 plus VAT may also apply to your new telephone land-line if there is no connection or the previous owner has retained their old number.

- Television cable offers vary between the main providers, NTL, Chorus and Sky Digital, but it is well worth researching your options and the price of various packages. Rural areas may not be as well serviced as urban areas and in some areas you may have to take out a digital satellite service instead of the more common multipoint microwave distribution (MMDS). Don't forget to register for your annual television licence (cost €152) with An Post.

Being a landlord

The tax implications of buying a buy-to-let property and becoming a landlord are examined in more detail in Chapter 4 see page 88. In the past decade thousands of properties in Ireland and abroad have been purchased for investment purposes – for both the rental income and capital gain. Not everyone is cut out to be a landlord however, and choose instead to use the services of a management company, foregoing a percentage of the rental income (which can amount to 10% or more) for the convenience of someone else collecting the rent, maintaining the property and dealing with tenants. There are a number of letting agencies available, including many of the larger estate agents.

If you do fancy the job yourself you need to tackle it in a professional manner. It isn't just bricks and mortar that you need to attend to – your tenants are your customers and deserve a quality product and good, on-going service.

To ensure the best return on your rental property consider the following:

- The property should be well designed, decorated and simply, but attractively furnished in simple, neutral colours (your tenant will want to put their own personal stamp on their home.)

- Kitchens and bathrooms in particular need to be pristine clean and should be well-equipped with sufficient crockery, glassware, utensils and new pots and pans.

- Heating, plumbing and appliances should be kept in top working order.
- Be prepared for repairs and renovations and create a realistic budget for this work.
- Keep a list of good, reliable tradesmen handy. Learn to do minor repairs yourself.
- Keep an itemised inventory of the contents of the property and ensure that your tenants have this list.
- Always ask for and check references from prospective tenants.
- Familiarise yourself with all your statutory legal responsibilities (see Chapter 4 for details) and those of your tenants.
- Ensure that you keep all receipts and records associated with your rental property (for accounting and tax purposes) and set up a separate bank account.
- You should inform your tenants, (if applicable) of any regular cleaning or maintenance schedule and of course, if there is an annual fee for this service. This might include annual carpet or curtain cleaning, the washing of outside windows and garden maintenance.
- Keep your sense of humour and a sense of proportion.

Rental yields

Successful landlords have realistic financial expectations. By the spring of 2005, the average annual yield from residential (as opposed to holiday home) rental properties in Ireland was estimated at c.2.5%, the lowest return in over a decade.

The fall in yield is mainly due to higher supply and emphasises the importance in choosing correct location for your rental property. Older apartments in particular have experienced the sharpest fall in yields, while tenants have become choosier about the type and style of apartment they will rent. Competition has resulted in the building of better and even larger apartments and a sharp improvement in the quality of fittings and decoration. Overall, capital appreciation is also falling with the average national property return expected to be in the (still healthy) region of 6%-7% per annum this year. For this reason you need to be particularly careful about buying a holiday home for investment purposes and you should not count on the rental yield to even meet your mortgage repayments.

Generous tax relief and low interest rates mean that buy-to-let investments continue to be financially attractive, but you still need to consider all the extra costs associated with being a landlord. These include:

- Vacant periods: most landlords factor in periods of up to at least six weeks a year when their property will be vacant as tenants move out and others move in.
- Repairs, on-going maintenance and re-decoration.
- Building and mortgage protection insurance and local authority service charges.
- Advertising and promotion.
- Annual service charges - especially in apartment complexes.
- Accountancy/tax advisory fees if you use a professional advisor to complete your annual tax return.

Legal responsibilities:

As a landlord you have certain legal obligations (as does your tenant) under the 2004 Residential Tenancies Act. Under the Act you not only have to be registered with the Revenue Commissioners and provide your tenant with a rent book or a written lease, and 28 days notice to quit, your property also has to meet certain minimum standards and provide security of tenancy once the tenant is in residence for more than six months. Rent can only be reviewed once a year unless there have been such changes or improvements during the year to merit another review.

This security of tenancy means that if your tenant has been in residence for at least six months then they can remain for the next three and a half years. The only terms under which you can terminate the lease is if the tenant doesn't comply with their obligations, the property doesn't suit them anymore – say it has become too small - you intend to sell the property within three months or undertake a major refurbishment or you want it for yourself or a family member.

Since disagreements can frequently arise between landlords and tenants there is a dispute resolution procedure in place through the Private Residential Tenancy Board, (tel. 01 888 2960) which was set up by the Department of the Environment in an effort to mediate disputes and save the parties expensive court appearances. For more details see page 91.

Being a property developer

Popular television programmes in which derelict, second hand properties are bought, renovated and sold on in a matter of weeks, earning the owner generous profits, have tempted many people to give up their day jobs to become property developers.

As anyone who has ever been an ordinary landlord can attest, there is nothing glamourous about dealing with tenants a who have locked themselves out of the house in the dead of night, or in replacing broken appliances – for the third time this year.

Buying and selling old property is a tough, dirty, frustrating and sometimes very lucrative business, but you need more than just a down payment and a sympathetic bank manager to make a success of it.

Instead, you need a myriad of skills, both practical and organisational to successfully project manage a rebuilding project. First, you need to have a good eye for properties with decent resale potential. Next, you need to know how to put together a detailed budget and business plan for your bank, to understand how the planning and building approval process works in your community and how to hire and supervise builders. Some personal building and decorating skills would also help, especially in keeping costs down.

Property development requires a strong nerve, especially in a high cost market like Ireland (where stamp duty and legal fees for second hand houses can add up to 10% automatically to your purchase price). A falling, let alone, static market, or a threat of rising interest rates can spell financial disaster if you are counting on a quick sale to finance your next project.

Most of all, say successful property developers, you need to remain emotionally detached from the houses you buy and renovate: property developing, like being a landlord, is a business, and should be treated that way.

All first time property developers make mistakes, but one of the biggest is to lose your objectively and to treat the development as if it is going to be your own home. It isn't. It is going to someone else's home and you don't want to impose your own taste (for swirly, patterned carpets or Spanish arches) that will have narrower appeal than a style and décor which is neutral and simple and that can be personalised by the new owner.

Since making money is the whole purpose of the exercise be careful about how much you spend on fittings and appliances. There is a happy medium between the cheapest kitchen taps on the market and the most stylish. How you decorate the property depends on its target market. Ripping out a bathtub in the only upstairs bathroom in a three-bedroom semi to install a high power glass and chrome shower unit that you always wanted, is probably going to eliminate families from your pool of buyers.

Before you set out your renovation and design plan be absolutely clear of not just the market for the property but the average price of houses or apartments on your street or neighbourhood. Spending €50,000 on an elaborate kitchen extension, if the value of the house doesn't merit that kind of investment, is a waste of money. Only undertake major renovations if you are certain they will create real profit.

Independent advice

Estate agents are not the best people to seek advice from when you are looking for a good property to develop. Naturally enough, they want to secure the best price for their client and the highest commission for their firm, and they will talk up even the worst features of the most derelict property.

If you are a novice developer try to get a second opinion from someone you trust with some kind of building or renovating experience, to view your short-list of properties. Listen carefully to what they say, and only then decide to proceed with a thorough, professional survey. As you become more experienced, you will be able to better trust your own instincts. Property development requires a strong nerve, especially in a high cost market like Ireland (where stamp duty and legal fees for second hand houses can add up to 10% automatically to your purchase price). A falling, let alone, static market, or a threat of rising interest rates can spell financial disaster if you are counting on quick sales to finance your next project.

Most of all, say successful property developers, you need to remain emotionally detached from the houses you buy and renovate: property developing, like being a landlord, is a business, and should be treated that way.

Ways to Survive a Property Crash

Is the global property market at sustainable growth levels? Is the house price bubble going to burst some day or is it already showing signs, at least here in Ireland, of gently deflating?

The ideal scenario is the soft landing option, say economists, which will cause the least disruption, especially to new buyers and speculators who may have over-borrowed to get onto the property ladder and are vulnerable to anything that will affect not just their ability to meet monthly mortgage repayments (like rising interest rates) but the re-sale value of their home. Even a sharp 'correction' in prices could push some buyers into 'negative equity', in which the market value of their home ends up being worth less than their mortgage.

There are ways to protect yourself from both a property market 'correction' or a full-blown meltdown:

- Accelerate your mortgage repayments now to reduce your debt and increase the amount of equity you own. If your house is currently worth €350,000, but you only own €50,000 worth of an equity in it or just over 14%, and prices drop 20% or €70,000, the market value of your house will drop to €280,000, but you will still owe the bank €300,000. This is negative equity.

- Spend less. During volatile or even uncertain economic times you should be doing your best to live within your means.

- Reduce your other debt. Use any savings earning low interest rates to pay off your most expensive debt – credit cards, hire purchase agreements and personal loans. Cut up the credit cards and learn to use cash again.

- Your house is a liability until it is paid off. Stop 'investing' any further in it until you own more equity in it, at least 30%, but ideally even more to provide a sufficient cushion in the event of a price downturn. If your house is currently valued at €350,000, this means you should own at least €105,000 worth of equity.

- Reduce your mortgage liability by renting a spare room in your house. The Rent a Room scheme allows you to earn €7,620 a year, tax-free, income that could be used to reduce your outstanding mortgage. Someone with a €200,000 mortgage will pay a total repayment of interest and capital of nearly €291,000 over the course of a typical 25 year mortgage. By taking on a lodger for five years, at a monthly charge of even €500 a month or €6,000 a year, you will reduce the term of the loan to just over 14 years and reduce the total capital and interest repayment to €249,000, a savings of €42,000.

Consider moving to a lower cost location. This sounds drastic, but homeowners who have built up considerable equity and are concerned about irrationally inflated property prices can secure their profit by downsizing. High re-purchase costs such as Stamp Duty and legal fees need to be factored into this contingency plan.

7
Property Statistics

The Statistics Game

Historically, property prices have slightly underperformed equities, that is, until recent years. Since the Millennium stock market crash of 2000, badly shaken investors who watched the value of their shares drop by nearly half, have shifted their money into property. Markets have only partly recovered since then but property values have soared.

As the Economist's house price index shows, here in Ireland average residential house prices increased by 179% between 1997 and 2004 and in the UK by 147%. In Spain and France, where the Irish are major second home investors, prices went up by 131% and 90% respectively. The United States, a regional, rather than national market, has seen house prices rise by a massive 65%; only once before has there been such a dramatic rise in American prices, during a relatively short period after World War two when thousands of soldiers returned home, ready to start families.

The following table tells an extraordinary tale in places like South Africa where prices are six percent higher over the previous year, Hong Kong where they have gone up by a whopping 30% (a clear indication that confidence has returned in the ex-colony); France, up 3.7% to 16% and the US, where in spite of rate rises during 2004, prices still increased by 3% on the previous year's high of 8.2%.

The Economist's house-price indices % Change on a year earlier			
	Q4 2004* %	Q4 2003 %	1997-2004 %
South Africa	29.6	23.4	195
Hong Kong	28.7	-1.1	-52
Spain	17.2	16.5	131
France	16.0	12.7	90
New Zealand	13.5	24.8	52
United States	11.2	8.2	65
China	10.8	5.1	na
UK	10.8	15.6	147
Sweden	9.8	6.1	76
Italy	9.7	10.6	65
Belgium	9.3	8.2	60
Ireland	8.5	13.7	179
Denmark	7.3	3.4	50
Canada	6.2	6.9	41
Netherlands	2.8	3.4	75
Australia	2.7	18.9	113
Switzerland	2.3	2.4	11
Singapore	0.9	-2.0	na
Germany	-1.3	-1.7	nil
Japan	-6.0	-5.7	-25
Sources: ABSA; Bulwien; ESRI; Japan Real Estate Institute; Nationwide; Nomisma; NVM; OFHEO; Quotable Value; Stadium; Swiss National Bank; government offices			

Spectacular as these house price increases have been, the fall in prices tells just as interesting a story: Australia has experienced the sharpest drop with house prices falling 16% in 2004, New Zealand by over 11% and and the UK by nearly 4%, a trend that has continued into 2005.

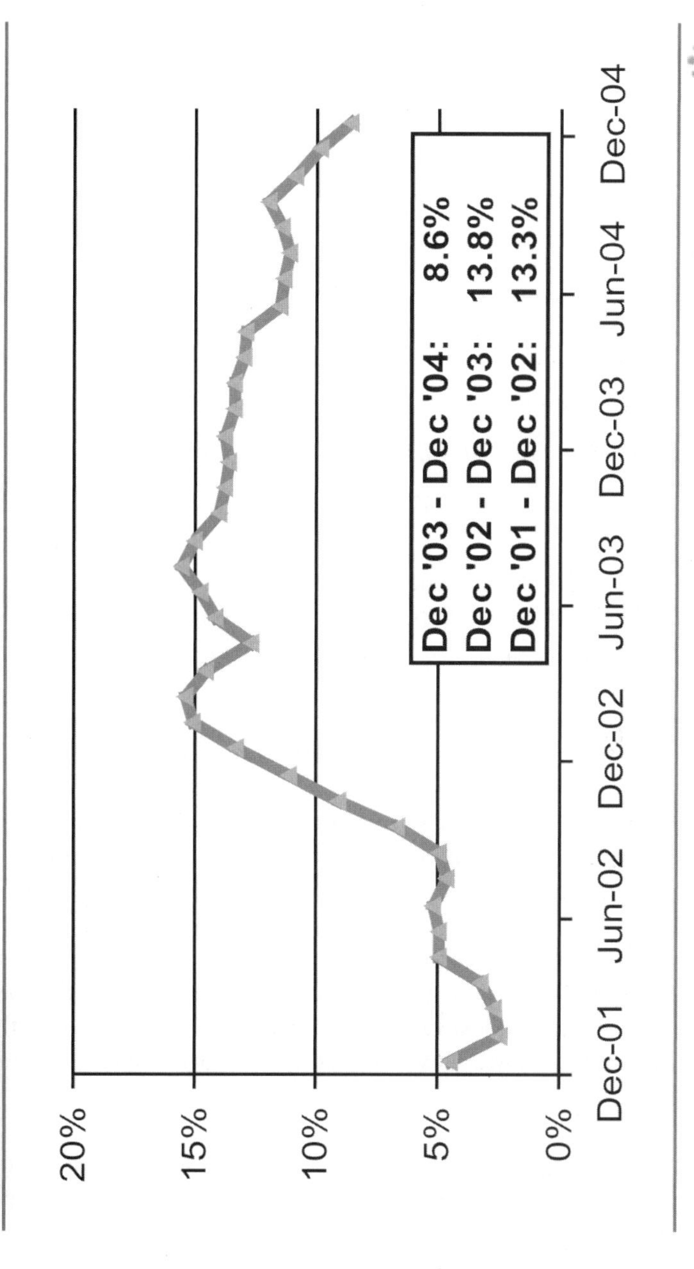
House Price Index
National House Prices
2004 annual growth rate significantly lower than previous two years.
20%
15%
10%
5%
0%
Dec-01
Jun-02
Dec-02
Jun-03
Dec-03
Jun-04
Dec-04
Dec '03 - Dec '04: 8.6%
Dec '02 - Dec '03: 13.8%
Dec '01 - Dec '02: 13.3%
permanent tsb

Irish prices slowing

As the graph on the previous page shows, Prices have slowed here since 2003 too. According to the permanent tsb/ESRI monthly House Price Index prices have fallen from 13.8% to 8.6% and their forecast is for a c.7% increase for 2005.

Two of the main reasons given for the boom here – a shortage of supply in the face of unprecedented demand by workers with higher earnings and thousands of newcomers looking for somewhere to live, and persistently low interest rates – are credible. Almost 50%, or 1.8 million of the population of 4.04 million is under 30.

Age Range of Irish Population of 4.04 million

Age	0 - 10	10 - 20	20 - 30	30 - 40	40 - 50	50 - 60	60+
%	14%	14%	17%	15%	13%	11%	15%

But, argues Robert Shiller, Yale professor of economics in the updated edition of his 2000 book 'Irrational Exuberance', this is only part of the story.

'Irrational Exuberance' is the term used by the US Federal Reserve chairman Alan Greenspan in 1996 to describe the overvalued American stock market. Shiller's book, which predicted the market's crash, came out in that same month, March 2000 and he is now convinced that the same pattern of speculative buying – this time of property – could result in a global property crash.

Shiller, and others, believes that "the notion that home prices always go up is very strong and very wrong" and that it is tied into the fact that ordinary people are now more conscious of property as capital, and believe that this capital defines their personal wealth and security. (A home, is no longer *just* a home.)

This heightened awareness is fuelled by endless property stories in the media, television programmes about property investing and word of mouth, says Shiller. As prices are 'talked up', concerns grows that unless you get on the property ladder immediately you will be priced out the market and this further fuels prices. Highly publicised resale values further encourage people to commit larger and larger amounts of their disposable income to servicing their mortgage.

Eventually, when properties become too expensive, causing a fall-off in first time buyers to feed the market – a feature of the sharp fall in Sydney, Australia where prices dropped by 16% last year – or because interest rates have shot up, as in the UK, prices fall. One of Shiller's concerns is that as prices fall, confidence falls, consumer spending falls, and there can be a domino effect in the wider economy.

Here, the situation only appears to be different in that demand remains strong by a large inward migration, a younger population, and by continuing low interest rates, which are controlled by Brussels and are dictated by the state of economic stagnation in Germany and France. Sufficient housing supply – 77,000 new homes were completed in 2004 - with demand still in or around 50,000 according to the ESRI means that soaring prices have finally ended. (Unfortunately for landlords, rental yields have also fallen.) Most economists believe that only a dramatic rise in rates or unemployment – and there is no immediate sign of either – will cause a property crash here.

What is clearly worrying however, is that any number of external events – illness or unemployment, part-time work due to starting a family, a slowdown in the world economy, could have drastic financial implications for anyone who is committing perhaps as much as half their take-home pay to servicing their mortgage.

For people with considerable value built up in their existing homes, the urge to leave these shores and to invest in cheaper markets in emerging EU countries or even further abroad is still proving to be irresistible. Millions of euro leave the country every month into overseas property that Irish investors believe will produce the kind of high capital returns that were achieved here during the last decade. Many expect their annual rental stream to pay some or all of their mortgage.

Euro property prices

According to the Economist survey property prices increased by 12.5% across Europe last year, though with glaring regional differences.

Spain and France saw the single highest increases of 17.2% and 16%, and have attracted huge interest from investors from high cost countries like Ireland and the UK. Investors are going much further afield, to places such as Bulgaria and Turkey, where prices are up as much as 30% in the past year. Investors should know however that Turkey for example has no double taxation agreement with Ireland.

The Economist strikes a warning chord regarding rental yields: the ratio of prices to rents was overvalued at the end of 2004 by 60% or more in places like the UK and Spain, by 46% in France. In some places, including the UK, says the Economist it makes more sense to rent and expensive property than to buy. That notion of 'dead' money being paid to a landlord no longer holds true every time.

Clearly, rents have been falling since 2003 as indicated by the following table. However, by the end of 2004 rents were stabilising and had started to pick up in the first quarter of 2005.

Average monthly rent for two-bed apartment			
	Sth Dublin	**Nth Dublin**	**West Dublin**
2003 Q1	**€1,581**	**€1,503**	**€1,155**
2003 Q2	**€1,472**	**€1,392**	**€1,137**
2003 Q3	**€1,334**	**€1,304**	**€1,107**
2003 Q4	**€1,311**	**€1,259**	**€1,082**
2004 Q1	**€1,271**	**€1,241**	**€1,076**
2004 Q2	**€1,281**	**€1,239**	**€1,033**
2004 Q3	**€1,219**	**€1,229**	**€1,027**
2004 Q4	**€1,219**	**€1,229**	**€1,027**
2005 Q1	**€1,231**	**€1,237**	**€1,035**

(Source: Gunne Residential)

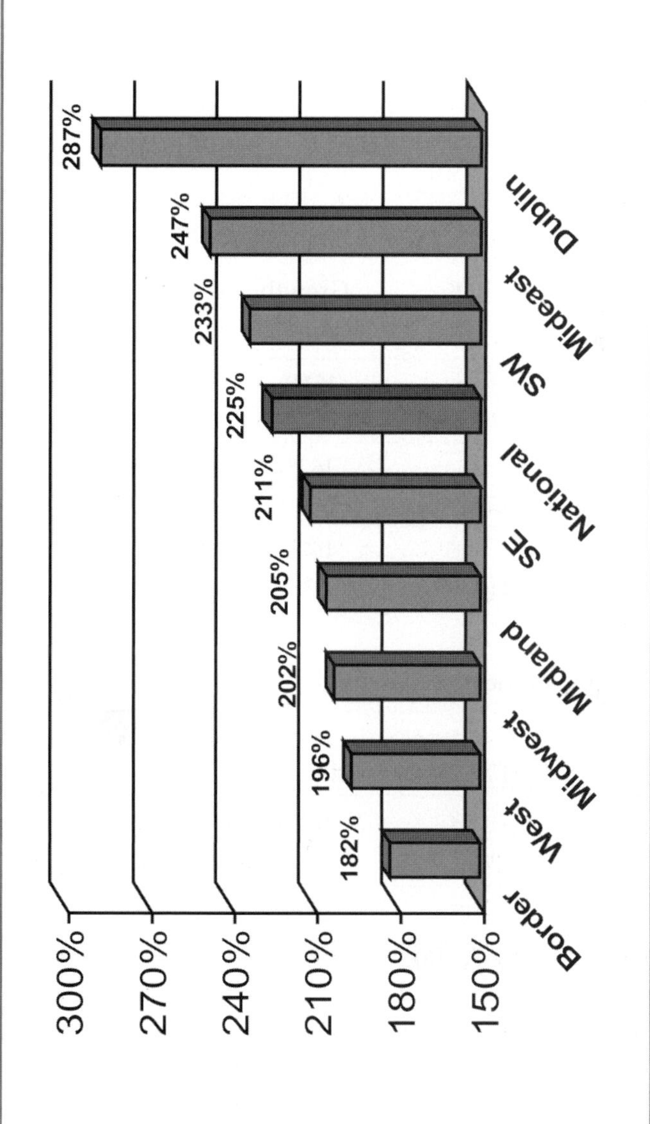
House Price Index
Regional House Price Growth since 1996
Dublin & Mideast continue to outstrip National growth, SW growth now also above other regions
300%
270%
240%
210%
180%
150%
287%
247%
233%
225%
211%
205%
202%
196%
182%
Dublin
Mideast
SW
National
SE
Midland
Midwest
West
Border
permanent tsb

Regional Price Variations

Regional price variations exist around the country as well. The top three counties for price growth purposes, according to the permanent tsb/ESRI House Price Index since 1996 are Donegal, Cork County and Offaly, while the bottom three are Kilkenny, Roscommon and Longford. The following table shows the sort of prices they have achieved and can be compared against the regional price growth graph.

Top 3 Counties by Growth to 2004 - by percentage and value				
	1996 €	**Growth '96 - 02**	**Growth '02 -'03**	**Growth '03 - 04**
Donegal	**(€61,463)**	**151% (€154,406)**	**12% (€172,408)**	**16% (€199,973)**
Cork County	**(€73,114)**	**167% (€195,029)**	**12% (€218,038)**	**16% (€252,850)**
Offaly	**(€61,146)**	**167% (€163,378)**	**11% (€181,852)**	**15% (€209,208)**
Bottom 3 Counties by Growth to 2004 - by percentage and value				
Kilkenny	**(€72,218)**	**157% (€185,287)**	**13% (€210,187)**	**9% (€228,282)**
Roscommon	**(€75,129)**	**105% (€154,273)**	**21% (€186,208)**	**7% (€198,533)**
Longford	**(€67,986)**	**139% (€162,740)**	**13% (€183,123)**	**5% (€193,106)**

(Source: PTSB / ESRI House Price Index)

As the graph shows the strongest regions for house price growth to the end of 2004 were Dublin and the mideast (which includes counties Kildare and Offaly) and the southwest, especially Cork.

The price differentiation is dramatic with Dublin achieving an accumulated percentage price increase of 287% over the eight years while the border areas, just 182%. Nevertheless, annualised, these are impressive returns, unlikely to be repeated going forward.

Property: the favoured asset of the rich

How much property do we actually own? Is it too much or too little? It has been estimated that the total value of residential property is now in the region of €240,000 billion, more than three times the value of the Irish stock exchange.

In a study in early 2005 of the investment portfolios of its wealthiest clients, NCB Stockbrokers determined that 55% of the average high net worth person's investment portfolio, worth an average of €3 million, is invested in property.

Property	Quoted Shares	Cash	Unquoted	Corporate Bonds
55%	28%	8%	6%	3%

Investor's private homes account for 42% of the value of their property assets; 20% is comprised of other residential holdings, while commercial, retail and industrial property account for an average of 27% of their holdings. The bulk of their property is held in Ireland with the UK accounting for 16% and continental Europe 5% of their holdings.

Of those surveyed, 15% said they had between 80% and 100% of their wealth in property, a further quarter said they held between 60% and 80% in bricks and mortar. Slightly more than half thought that their property was 'over valued', half those surveyed said they were considering increasing their property assets.

Index

I

J

L

M

O

P

Q

R

S

T

U

V

W

Y

Useful References

An Bord Pleanala
64 Marlborough Street
Dublin 1
Tel: 01 858 8100
www.pleanala.ie

Department of the Environment and Local Government
Custom House,
Dublin 1
Tel: 1890 20 20 21
www.environ.ie

The Irish Credit Bureau
ICB House,
Newsteed,
Clonskeagh,
Dublin 14

Irish Auctioneers and Valuers Institute
38 Merrion Square
Dublin 2
Tel:661 1794
www.realestate.ie

ESB Networks
Tel: 1850 372 372
www.esb.ie

Bord Gais
Tel: 1850 427532
www.bge.ie

Private Residential Tenancies Board
Canal House,
Canal Road,
Dublin 1
www.prtb.ie

Threshold (housing agency)
19 Mary's Abbey
Dublin 7

Tel. 01-872 6311
www.threshold.ie

Revenue Commissioners
Tel. 01-878 0100
www.revenue.ie

HomeBuyHomeSell
(Conveyancing Service)
www.homebuyhomesell.ie

Smart Telecom
Tel: 1800 931300
www.smartelecom.ie

NTL Ireland
Tel: 1800 321321
www.ntl.com/locales.ie

Eircom
Tel: 1850 203 204
www.eircom.ie

Chorus
Tel: 1890 202029
www.chorus.ie

ESAT BT
Tel: 1890 924924
www.esatbt.ie

Internet Addresses for Letting Agents

www.homelocators.ie
www.hookemacdonald.ie
www.irishhomeminders.ie
www.myhome.ie
www.rletts@lisney.com
www.daft.ie

Holiday Letting Agents

www.activeireland.ie
www.country-holidays.ie
www.irishlets.net
www.selfcateringireland.ie

Removal Companies

Allen Removals and Storage
Greenhills Road
Tallaght
Dublin 24
Tel: 01 451 3585
www.allenremovals.ie

Maquire International Moving and Storage
5 Albert Avenue
Bray
Co Wicklow
Tel: 01 276 1700
www.info@maquireinternational.ie

Oman Removals
10 South Link Park
Frankfield, Cork
Tel: 1850 668464
www.sales@oman.ie

Glossary of Terms

APR

This stands for annual percentage rate - the annual rate of interest charged on a loan. It takes account of all the costs involved over the full term of the loan, such as any setup charges and the interest rate. It provides one of the best means of comparing the cost of different types of credit.

Bridging Loan

This is a short-term loan given by a lending institution to 'bridge' a time difference between buying a new home and selling your existing home. This loan is then paid off when the current property is sold.

Collateral

Property or some other asset used as security for a loan

Conveyancing

Technical term for the legal process of buying, selling and mortgaging a property.

Deeds

The legal document by which legal title to freehold and leasehold property is transferred from the seller to the buyer.

Default

Failure to pay some or all installments due on a mortgage or other loan.

Deposit

The amount, usually around 10% of the house purchase price.

Equity

Net value of your home calculated by subtracting the outstanding mortgage owing from the current market value.

Equity Release

Equity is the difference between the amount of money a person owes on their mortgage and the current value of their home. Equity Release allows you to borrow up to 90% of the current value of you home, for a number of different purposes.

Freehold

The owner of the property owns the property without payment of any rent and without a limit in time.

Guarantor

A person who agrees to pay the borrowers debt if the mortgage holder defaults (fails to pay).

HB47

The Home Bond Scheme Certificate provided by your builder. The aim of this scheme is to protect new houses against structural defects and to ensure that property standards are maintained in the house building industry.

Indemnity Bond

An insurance policy, in favour of your lender, to cover any shortfall that might arise between the amount owing and the value of your home if you default. An indemnity bond is usually required when you are borrowing more than a certain percentage of the purchase price - e.g. 75%. Many lenders waive this fee for first-time buyers.

Irish Credit Bureau

A credit reference agency that maintains a database of individual credit histories and ratings. You can obtain a copy of your own details for a small fee by contacting the ICB on (01) 260 0388 or download a form from **www.oasis.gov.ie**.

Land Registry

A Government body that records ownership of property.

Legal Charge

A legal document conferring legal ownership of the mortgagor's (borrowers) estate to the lender, while allowing the mortgagor to remain in possession and to use the property with the right to redeem legal ownership, which is called equity of redemption.

Leasehold Property

The purchaser owns the property buy pays ground rent annually and is subject to the terms of the lease.

Letter of Offer

Also called the 'offer of advance' this is a formal statement by the lender of the amount they are prepared to lend you.

Loan-to-Value (LTV)

This is a percentage size of the loan based on the value of the property. E.g. If you owe €50,000 and you home is worth €200,000, your LTV is 25%.

Mortgage Protection

This is a term life insurance product, which lenders are legally obliged (except in limited circumstances) to ensure you have in place. It pays off the outstanding amount due on your mortgage if you die. You are free to shop around for the best rates and do not have to accept the lenders' product or recommendation.

Mortgage protection insurance should not be confused with mortgage repayment protection, which provides cover for a certain number of installments in the event that you fall ill, have an accident or become unemployed.

Mortgage Repayment Cover

This ensures that your mortgage repayments are met for a period of up to 12 months, following an accident, sickness or redundancy.

Negative Equity

This occurs when the amount owing on your house is higher than the market value.

Redemption

The word used to describe a mortgage when it is repaid.

Searches

Your solicitor will undertake searches to confirm that the seller of a property can pass ownership to you and that there are no outstanding judgments or liens (outstanding debt) against the property.

Split Rate (Mix & Match)

Here you can set a part of your mortgage at a fixed rate and the remainder at a variable rate. If rates fall, the repayments on the variable part of your mortgage will reduce, and if rates rise you have the security of knowing that only the variable payment is affected.

Tenure

Type of ownership of property e.g. Freehold, leasehold.

Title Deeds

The documents showing the ownership of the property.

NOTES

NOTES

NOTES

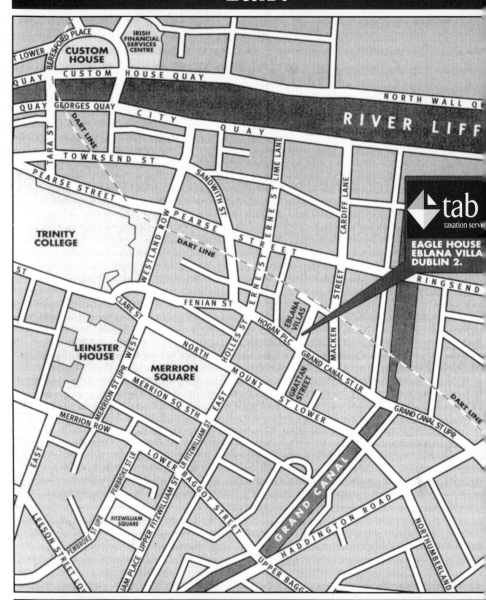